*V*IRGINS

AND OTHER ENDANGERED SPECIES

A MEMOIR

VIRGINS
AND OTHER ENDANGERED SPECIES
A MEMOIR

DOROTHEA STRAUS

Moyer Bell

Wakefield, Rhode Island & London

Published by Moyer Bell

The author gratefully acknowledges the following publications in which parts of this book first appeared: "Demons and Other Supernatural Presences" in a slightly altered form in *Partisan Review* and part in *Small Press* magazine; "Epitaph" in a slightly altered form in the *Partisan Review*; and "Family Doctor" in *MD* magazine; "The Bachelor" in *Fiction* magazine; "The Friend of Brahms" in *Confrontation*.

Excerpts from *The Assistant* by Bernard Malamud, copyright © 1957, and copyright renewed © 1985 by Bernard Malamud. Reprinted by permission of Farrar, Straus & Giroux, Inc.

First Edition

LIBRARY OF CONGRESS
CATALOGING-IN-PUBLICATION DATA

Straus, Dorothea.
    Virgins and other endangered species / Dorothea Straus.
        p.   cm.
    ISBN 1-55921-118-0
    1. Straus, Dorothea—Biography. 2. Authors, American—20th century—Biography. I. Title.
PS3569.T6918Z477   1993
813'.54—dc20
[B]   92-39803
                                                             CIP

Printed in the United States of America

Distributed by Publishers Group West, Box 8843, Emeryville, CA 94662, 1-800-788-3123 (in California 1-510-658-3453) and Pandemic Ltd. in Europe

FOREWORD

I present a fine case of colored hearing. Perhaps, hearing is not quite accurate since the color sensation seems to be produced by the very act of orally forming a given letter while I imagine its outline. The long *a* of the English alphabet has for me the tint of weathered wood . . . oatmeal *n*, noodle limp *l* and the ivory-backed mirror of *o* . . . Passing on to the blue group, there is steely *x*, thundercloud *z* and huckleberry *k* . . . *s* is a curious mixture of azure and mother-of-pearl . . . in the green group there are alder leaf *f*, the unripe apple of *p* and pistachio *t* . . . the yellows comprise *e's* and *i's*, creamy *d*, bright golden *y* and *v* . . . Finally, among the reds, *b* has the tone called burnt sienna by painters, *m* is a fold of pink flannel . . .

Vladimir Nabokov, *Speak Memory*

Since I see letters in ordinary black on white, I can lay no claim to the rainbow alphabet created by the hallucinations of the quirky genius of Nabokov. But, a word, a phrase, a paragraph and, more frequently, a book title, may separate itself from the mass, clothed in indelible color. For this reason, I continue to be offended by the mistranslation of Marcel Proust's *A La Recherche du Temps Perdu* into the sentimental sachet lavender of *Remembrance of Things Past*. And I rejoiced, recently, at the sight of a new Modern Library edition of Proust with his original title: *In Search of Lost Time*, proclaiming at last in the English language the purpose of his work.

For years, Proust has been my guru. But when I study a portrait of him I find no hint of his power there. I am confronted, instead, by a dandy with a dapper mustache and soft, sensuous lips, fashioned, it seems, to sip Champagne. He is in evening dress and wears a white orchid in his buttonhole in preparation for his night rounds to the aristocratic salons of Paris; or, perhaps, it may be that he is on his way to some homosexual brothel: a half-Jew, a member of the bourgeoisie, he lacks the social credentials for the first, and his frail constitution and over-sensitive nervous system are strangely at odds with the second. An outsider, he is drawn to these two worlds by the extravagance of his snobbery and the exacerbated perversity of his instincts. It is useless to remind myself that many Catholic saints were flawed—I am not attracted to weaknesses in my prophets. Yet it is the work of Proust, read and reread through a lifetime, that has sustained me more than any other.

It is he who made me aware that the act of deliberate remembrance is weak, kin to forgetfulness; it abandons the past and its inhabitants to the grave. Only through *involuntary* memory, induced by the five senses, does a miracle occur and the layered years give up their submerged treasure of people and places. With the proverbial *madeleine* (little cake), Proust's childhood summers return to him, and the underlying theme is evoked, resounding like the peal of an organ, starting the chain of recall that links the many volumes of *A La Recherche Du Temps Perdu*, (*In Search of Lost Time*); an experiment in memory, pursued and confirmed.

> . . . And once I had recognized the taste of the crumb of the madeleine soaked in her concoction of lime flowers which my aunt used to give me—immediately the old gray house upon the street where her room was, rose up like the scenery of a theatre to attach itself to the little pavilion opening on the garden—with the house, the town, from morning to night in all weather, the square where I was sent before luncheon, the streets along which I used to run errands, the country roads we took when it was fine . . . The Japanese amuse themselves by filling a porcelain bowl with water and steeping in it little crumbs of paper which until then are without character or form; but the moment they become wet, stretch themselves and bend, take on color and distinctive shape, become flowers or houses or people, permanent and recognizable, so in that moment all the flowers in our garden and M. Swann's park and the waterlilies on the Vivonne and the good folk of the village and their little dwellings and the parish church and the whole of Cambray and its surroundings taking their proper shapes and growing solid, spring into being, town and garden, alike, from my cup of tea . . . [1]

Enlightened by this philosophy of secular immortality, indebted to the Master (novelist, poet, scientist of memory), I see the name he gave his work, a personal, imperishable universe in book form, glowing with the vibrant, prismatic hues of fine stained glass.

The passage of time has its own mysterious erratic pace: the years may be counted but their density cannot be measured. Tonight I find myself the oldest person at a gathering, yet it seemed that only last season I was the youngest person in the room. Just as someone riding an escalator, without self-propulsion, is moved to another level, I had been transported to my present status through the stealthy progress of time. Yet, in compensation for this unavoidable melancholy transit, it can happen that buried moments, unbidden, may be reasserted, ushered in by those bodily herald angels: hearing, sight, smell, taste and touch, available to all. It was Proust who alerted me to these revelations empowered to penetrate the opaque veil of Now. Who can argue that this is not metaphysics of a kind—a temporary conquest over death? It is a primary satisfaction, occasionally, to capture one of those transcendental twinges, to commemorate it upon the page.

For the sake of an imposed order, I have grouped the chapters of this book, devoted to mnemonics, under headings: The Day Before Yesterday and Yesterday realizing that clock and calendar, too, are arbitrary and approximate. My subjects, for the most part, are representatives of extinct genera—dinosaurs—who once impressed their footprints upon the territory of my brain.

THE
DAY
BEFORE
YESTERDAY

Chapter One

THE BACHELOR

Whenever I pass the dilapidated docks still jutting into the Hudson River on New York's West Side, I recall the moment when I discovered that my father was a bachelor.

Recently, there has been some attempt to revive the piers, replacing the stately floating luxury hotels that once sailed from these berths to ply their dignified routes, back and forth across the Atlantic, with the insignificance of cruise ships bound for tropical resorts. But, just as cosmetic surgery cannot change a commoner into a queen, despite the restorations, the docks have lost the power over my imagination that they once held.

European travel was ushered in by the hoarse, reverberating, penetrating blast of the foghorn, both thrilling and menacing as a call to battle. But I relied on the reassuring nearness of my father, as we stood together at the railing of the Promenade Deck, watching, far below on the dock, the myriad, tiny faces of the crowd, gesticulating wildly, waving handkerchiefs in farewell. After the "All visitors ashore" call, I felt the engine, the great heart of the ship, starting up beneath my feet, and, hand-in-hand, my father and I stepped over the raised iron threshold, into the Art Deco lounge. We descended the grand staircase (still stationary, soon it would rise and fall, and we, by turn, would be rendered leaden or weightless, according to the pitch and roll of the ship) as we followed the maze of corridors to our cabins. They were cluttered with *bon voyage* baskets of fruit and candy—coals to Newcastle—as the ship itself was a cornucopia of plenty. My mother's tastes were frugal, and we found her, with the help of our loyal French maid, Alice, clearing out the glut, distributing the redundant gifts among the stewards and stewardesses—the flowers, in haste, because my mother believed that their heavy perfume poisoned the atmosphere of the cabin, interfering with a healthful night's sleep. Furthermore we would not have the benefit of much tonic sea air, as the portholes could be opened only a crack, and they were small, like round eyes without pupils, in which the blankness of sea and sky alternated; framed in iron, offering only a blind stare. It was as though the designers of the vessel had wished to minimize our vision of the elements, reducing the vast Atlantic that the mighty liner would consume in its wake in a mere week's time. Every now and then, Alice, who had a sweet tooth, would surreptitiously slip a packet of candy into her pocket; while my brother, who collected everything, indiscriminately, would grab as much as he could from the disappearing donations. The restlessness of travel made my mother nervous and I knew she preferred the summers spent in the country in a rented house, not too far from home, available to friends and the good conversations which she craved. My father was unsociable, requiring only the company of his immediate family, and he thrived on the stimulation of foreign places, preferably urban.

This voyage promised to be no different from all the others, following the same rituals. As we were being tugged slowly out of the harbor, my father and I mounted the stairs again to view the Statue of Liberty, her torch held high. In the reverse of her welcome, she now blessed departure, a return to the Old World. And, just as the sound of a military band may cause a meaningless lump of emotion in the throat, and tears in the eyes of the least chauvinistic, pacifist spectator, the Statue of Liberty assured me, who normally took my place of birth for granted, that mine was the best country in the universe, making leave-taking poignant and lending to travel an aura of high adventure.

In my memory, embarking always took place at noon, so, soon it was in order to descend to the great dining hall, trellised in gold moldings and hung with crystal chandeliers. Here, the architects had been at their most successful in the exclusion of the out-of-doors. There were no windows, of any kind, to remind us that we were at sea; nor could we hear the faintest sound of waves, only the tinkle of glass and china, and at dinner, a string orchestra playing those sadly seductive Viennese waltzes that made me yearn for the romance I had never experienced. During a storm, the Atlantic took revenge against its banishment, and the dining room became the location for the most acute pangs of sea-sickness. When the sea was rough, we rarely ventured into the dining room, but lay stretched out on our berths, listening sympathetically to the protesting groans and creakings of the hinges in our cabins. Only my father never skipped a meal. Sometimes, his health and good humor would prevail upon me and I would brave the deck, but the fear of being actively sick in public soon made me scurry back to the privacy of the cabin. Now, when I smell that odor, amalgam of salt sea spray, brass polish and linoleum—even on dry land—I am invaded again by those far-off pangs connected with the Atlantic crossings by ships whose names are no longer heard.

It was on the first afternoon "out" that I made my discovery. Tea and gingersnaps were being served and from my lounge chair, I watched the passengers, like merry-go-round horses, taking their constitutionals around and around the promenade deck. Travel had trained me to be a sharp observer of people; and, just as a skilled hunter can sight his prey, no celebrity on board escaped the acuteness of my vision. From far off I spotted her, the actress I shall call, Ida Bright. I had seen her on stage in those drawing-room dramas, extinct today, and she was familiar, also, from newspaper and magazine photographs. That afternoon she was dressed in a costume of *bois de rose*, (an old-fashioned color—a cross between pink and beige); matching flannel suit, stockings, shoes, gloves and tight-fitting cloche hat, from which two golden points of flapper's hair escaped to caress her rouged cheeks. She was middle-aged, but to my eyes, because she was "theatre" and famous, she had more attraction, by far, than the bloom of young womanhood; which, to me, a ten year old, seemed as remote as the late maturity of Ida Bright. To my consternation and joy, she halted in front of my father's chair, exclaiming, "Alfred! I can't believe it. How wonderful to see you again!"

My father evinced no enthusiasm. On the contrary,

if his swarthy complexion had permitted a blush, he would have turned red as any embarrassed school boy.

After introducing her husband, the actress continued, "We must meet for cocktails this evening."

But my awkward parent merely muttered something unintelligible, and, her amiable overtures rebuffed, Ida Bright moved off.

My mother, usually unstinting in her admiration for my father, reprimanded him, "You didn't have to be so rude. Is she a friend from your bachelor days?"

"Bachelor days." I had heard the phrase used by various relatives in reminiscences and anecdotes about my father. But, although the word bachelor conjured up in my imagination a swashbuckling figure on the order of D'Artagnan in *The Three Musketeers*, until that moment I had never applied it to my father's past. As far as I was concerned, his life began with my first awareness of him. What happened prior to that was nebulous, unbelievable, as the idea of any existence before my birth. The only evidence I had of my father's early days was a photograph of his graduating class at Columbia College's School of Mines, in which he sits in the front row, altogether unrecognizable and unpleasing, with a shock of dark hair, a narrow face and large protruding ears—all totally unrelated to the comfortably plump, balding presence to which I was accustomed.

"Why is it that you always keep every interesting person you used to know away from me?" my mother continued.

In retrospect, I cannot decide whether this was asked in protest, wistfully or in jest. But I realize now that after his late marriage, just as a retired general may be relieved to find himself in mufti, my father joyfully discovered the ease of Victorian carpet slippers—the safety and comforts of home—while my mother, a woman of her time with limited experience of the world, dwelled with pride on her husband's former conquests, which seemed to her like so many medals of victory.

As for me, it was on that Altantic crossing, at the encounter with Ida Bright, one of those apocryphal actress companions made material, that I began to concern myself with my father as bachelor. And since our views of others are always subjective and, therefore, inaccurate, perhaps my imaginings were no more untrue than my memories. In any case, I preserve both against the destructiveness of time: They are my inheritances.

Due to the monotony of shipboard life, the days moved slowly; despite the fact that as we sailed towards Europe, watches were set forward, one hour in every twenty-four. Yet the acceleration was discreet, barely noticeable, and, as in a great cradle, the voyagers were rocked gently in time, as well as in space.

My father continued to avoid Ida Bright and soon she gave up and I grew resigned to my habitual role of passive observer. At night, the actress wore black, her naked back, powdered white, exposed by the low cut of her evening gown held up by narrow rhinestone shoulder straps; another fine diamond circlet crossed her brow; her brilliants glinted, in concert with the showy dazzle of the dining room chandeliers, like small deposits fallen from large planets. In the Art Deco lounge, as she sat with her husband and privileged friends, smoking a cigarette in a long holder, she was as sleek as a picture in a fashion magazine—and as inaccessible. Across the obstacles of small tables, through the potted palms, we nodded, good-evening, and that was all.

My father, an inveterate tourist, was generally regarded as cosmopolitan, as much European as American. Even my mother claimed that when he traveled in Spain, he was often taken for a Spaniard. Perhaps, that is why a full-scaled reproduction of an Infanta by Velazquez was placed over my father's bed in our apartment.

Yet my father had been born in Brooklyn, inside a brewery compound transported from Germany in the emigration of 1848. German was spoken at home and it was the language of his first school, inside the brewery yard, attended by eighteen cousins and the children of neighboring German-American brewers, taught by a master, imported from the "old country." In this snug, industrious enclave, my father's family was integrated. Assimilated Jews for three generations, they created their own traditions, the brewing industry and their atheism, in repudiation of the ancient history of their ancestors. When my grandparents, in their old age, left the shelter of the brewery yard in Brooklyn to move to New York City, it was as though they had undertaken an emigration more dislocating than the former. In an apartment on the fashionable upper East Side, they were no longer German-Americans among German-Americans, but Jews, become doubly alien—to Christians as well as to a society of their own kind, with which they had never mingled. I picture them perched, unnaturally high, above the street: my rosy-cheeked, white-bearded, blue-eyed grandfather who resembled a proper German burgher and his dark, diminutive wife, a meticulous housekeeper who was also reputed to be able to recite by heart German classic poetry. In New York City they became wealthy greenhorns. Too old to partake of this other environment, they were solaced in their loneliness by strong family ties, comforted by the transposition of the massive, claw-footed Jacobean furniture from their home in Brooklyn, the nostalgic aromas of German cooking—pot roast and potato pancakes—and the taste and texture, the reassuring excellence of their own brew.

When my father was a young man, he felt the challenge of the change in locale. Discarding the pride of the family, he left his elder brother and sundry relatives to run the business, while he became an engineer. And, just as the bridges and railroads he designed spanned geographical distance, the lesser mileage of the move to New York City opened vistas of new, sophisticated pleasures. The family unity in atheism he retained, polishing his non-belief like a shield. And, just as a religious man may insist upon dogma, my father, a bigot of the rational, the material, was intolerant of even the slightest hint of mysticism.

In later years he used to warn me, "Religion is the crutch of the weak."

A youthful dandy, brandishing his stylish walking stick and equipped with a sensuous *joie de vivre*, a lover of beauty and luxury, a lavish giver with a strong penchant for the "weaker sex," my father, a bachelor of the "gilded age," set out to conquer.

For the purpose of the portrait of my father as a young blade, I shall call my subject by his first name: Alfred. And for the initial sitting, I will place him at the site of his bachelor's flat: *The Alwyn Court* apartments, still standing today, outwardly unchanged. How many times I have examined its walls, thickly encrusted with gargoyles—stone dragons, reptiles, toads and imps—as if by some sorcery, they might divulge Alfred's secrets to me. The building is situated on Seventh Avenue, one block north of Carnegie Hall and around the corner from the Plaza, an area haunted for me by the horse-drawn carriages that continue to solicit trade. The ancient, toothless coachmen recalled from my childhood have been replaced by young hippie-type drivers, with long, tangled androgynous locks, but their top hats have been purloined from their predecessors. This area teases me with the past, as if the scene enduring from another century were granting me a stay on my own mortality. I have even ventured inside the narrow, dark enclosure of the *Alwyn Court* apartments, but a security guard chased me away. Not, however, before I had listened to the splashing of a fountain and wondered whether it had sounded the same to Alfred and the bachelors who shared this home: Joseph, a cousin, black sheep of the family because he remained idle in the midst of their industry; and Edward Steichen, the famous photographer in an earlier incarnation. But chiefly, I search out Alfred in the sunless court, with its jet of water that harbors in its persisting slender fall echoes of another age.

As I begin to paint the image of Alfred, a bachelor, someone I never met, it is only against his former haunts or those I fancy resemble them that my subject emerges. I select the scarlet and mauve pigment of the *bel epoque* for the restaurant in London, Paris or New York, where I place my model at a well-positioned table for two, opposite a lady, often an actress, who glows softly in the candlelight, shielded by a rosy, pleated shade. Sometimes, she has pinned, artfully, a corsage of orchids or camellias to her evening gown, near, but not concealing the cleavage of her breasts, and, if she is a favorite, a chain with a jewel pendant may encircle her graceful throat—gifts from her escort. She is usually blond and has a small nose. Alfred, unlike many of his contemporaries, is clean shaven, his swarthy skin fragrant from after-shave lotion. He considers himself homely but his attraction for women (over and above his generosity) is undeniable. It raises his self-esteem. Do they find his elfin looks exotic? More likely, they are warmed by the understanding and humor in his small green eyes. Chiefly, I believe, it is his genuine appreciation of their sex that draws them; just as an enthusiastic connoisseur of art before a Manet or a Degas, Alfred, in the presence of a chosen beauty was able to lose himself.

The *Ziegfeld Follies* is only a name today, but it is still possible to visualize the high-stepping girls in their perky can-can skirts, or in feathered headdresses and long slitted gowns with fishtail trains, their uniformly perfect legs, performing on the stage of a theatre whose parterre is stuffed in red velvet, while overhead, gilded boxes crawl beneath a ceiling of heaven blue where cherubs float as plentiful as clouds in an expectant twilight. This species of architecture lingers, but it is being supplanted by the austerities of modern design. The out-moded theatres are largely the work of Harry Hertz, Alfred's classmate who sits beside him in the front row in that graduation photograph, conspicuous because of his craggy, handsome head. Later, during my childhood, I met him but rarely. He was by then a tall

cadaver, a wreck, with twitching features, wearing a mon-
ocle that danced a jig to the rhythm of his facial jerkings.
Although it was never mentioned openly, I gathered,
somehow, that Harry was hopelessly addicted to drugs, an
undisclosed disease, and that his wife and sons were finan-
cially dependent on Alfred. Although no one discussed this
private charity in my presence, in the way of children,
through some osmosis of which their parents are unaware,
I learned the facts. Also, I had heard people exclaiming,
"What a tragedy! All that talent gone to waste. A brilliant
career thrown out because of that terrible weakness!"

When I enter the shabby yet festive atmosphere of
a turn-of-the-century theatre, I am followed by the spirits
of two men-about-town: Alfred and Harry. They often
frequented the *Ziegfeld Follies*, from which Alfred plucked
one of the dancing girls. She alone of all his ladies survived
to enter my life, and from the face of an old woman, I was
sometimes able to reconstruct the pert features of her youth.
Alfred's affair must have been short-lived because he
introduced her to Harry Hertz and she promptly fell in love
with his good looks and the glamour of his successful career
as a theatre architect. It is probable that Alfred relinquished
her without much pain because I believe that, like the
conventional Edwardian dandy he was, relationships with
actresses, chorus girls in particular, no matter how delicious,
were not to be taken too seriously. He must have been
stunned when his friend gave up freedom and general
popularity to marry Rosie, while Alfred continued to go his
bachelor ways.

Only when he visited his old parents in the confines
of their New York City home did he take on another

guise—or rather it was assumed for him. While looking forward eagerly to his arrival, it was impossible for them to see him as other than their younger son, descendant from a line of solid brewers. True, he had always been a touch unruly; and his mother enjoyed telling the story of Alfred, aged seven, running off with an organ grinder and monkey who used to perform in the brewery yard. After a frantic twenty-four-hour search, Alfred had been retrieved but they had learned as little about this escapade as they had about his present life. Certainly, his parents would have given no credibility to the polo playing, yachting parties, membership in artists' clubs and, especially, to his actress-mistresses. It is doubtful that they would have recognized their son on the bridle paths of Central Park, booted and spurred, astride a thoroughbred, with a lovely woman in a long skirt riding side-saddle at his side.

When Alfred called on members of his family, he usually had a present in hand. At the red brick house of his brother, Julius, overlooking Brooklyn's Prospect Park, there were already two nephews and a niece to acclaim their uncle who came bearing expensive toys. For Alfred's parents there were hot-house fruits and vegetables, out of season, and those dainty, small cakes called "lady fingers." His mother, for whom he was the favorite child, would grumble, "so much extravagance . . . ," while she bustled to the kitchen to tell the cook to include these delicacies with the heavy meal of pot roast and potato pancakes. Yes, Alfred might be a bit irregular and he certainly spent too much money, but they asked no questions, knowing only that he came to them from a wider world beyond their parlor; and for this very reason, he was welcomed all the more warmly there.

But Alfred was growing tired of variety and change and he began to consider the stability of marriage and children. As he walked along Fifth Avenue at a brisk pace, swinging his cane like a metronome to set the rhythm of his steps, he contemplated with pleasure the façades—Baroque, Rococo, Georgian, Gothic—of the mansions on his route. He was interested in the histories of these houses, their construction as well as the names of their architects and occupants. But always a realist, he entertained no dreams of a comparable neo-royal domesticity for himself. Rather, the sight of Fifth Avenue's nineteenth-century palaces merely firmed him in the quest for the bourgeois comforts of a home of his own. Yet none of the women he knew was a possible candidate for wife. Although he was not an ambitious snob, he did require breeding and culture as well as physical beauty, and his position on the fringe of the city's German-Jewish society of his day limited his choice. At forty, he was still a bachelor.

But romantic love, like sudden success or failure, all life's sharp turning points, depends in part on chance; startling us by its unexpectedness and the unlikelihood of its hiding place. Therefore, when Alfred arrived at a reception given by a cousin and his wife, member of a prominent Jewish family, the gathering seemed no more auspicious than others he had occasionally attended, engendering in him that same combination of boredom and unease. With the assimilated Jew's deprecation of his kind, he wondered at the apparent complacency, even arrogance, of these guests, limited to a homogenous, segregated group. And he was glad that he carried an invisible ticket admitting him to the livelier conglomeration of artists.

Suddenly, he was startled out of these musings. He had sighted across the room his ideal of womanly beauty—a vision, all in white, slender, wasp-waisted, full bosomed, with abundant wheat blond hair. She was aristocratic yet animated, and she also possessed the necessary symmetry of features—wide-set eyes, delicate nose, a heart-shaped face with high cheekbones and modeled chin. To Alfred's eyes, the puffy sleeves of her shirtwaist were the folded wings of a Bernini angel. He made his way to where she stood.

A few weeks later, following tea at the Edwardian Room of the Plaza Hotel, he hired a horse and closed carriage for a ride through Central Park. In the swaying interior that smelled unromantically of horse manure, stale tobacco from the coachman's cigar, musty upholstery and another odor, undefined, faintly disreputable, and to the serenading of hooves upon asphalt, Alfred took his prize into an expert embrace. At that instant, as with the wave of a magic wand, the bachelor was miraculously transformed and the prospective husband and father emerged.

In his old age, my father used to say, in a tone uncharacteristically detached and ruminative for a man of action, "My marriage was only a small island in my life."

And it was true. It had been preceded by twenty years of bachelorhood, and although my mother was eleven years his junior, he was to survive her by twenty years more. He mourned her loss, her untimely death, and never ceased to hold her up as a model of perfection—her beauty, brains, her articulate brilliance laced with wit (gallows humor, I believe now, because melancholy, a featureless pursuer was never far away)—and her unselfishness. My father, to the end, remained a *bon vivant*, even as the light on the landscape changed, and although he was protected by a carapace of healthy self-interest, in his relationships he gave and received much human warmth.

In the apartment where I grew up, in which my father now lived alone, there was only one bridal photograph of my mother, almost unrecognizable, less a likeness of an individual than a symbol trussed in satin folds disfigured by an unbecoming May Day wreath of orange blossoms. The reproduction of the Velazquez Infanta still hung above my father's bed. This odd tribute to him from my mother spoke to me of her love for him and helped me to recapture her face.

Late in life, after the death of his partner in engineering, my father entered the family business. Although he took pleasure in his daily work and his authority and could wax sentimental about the long history of the brewery, he never became the plodding burgher, leaving that role to his brother. Rather, my father returned to his bachelor habits. On Saturday afternoons, he visited the auction galleries, where his dapper dress, bow tie from Sulka's, bowler, walking stick and his regular attendance caused the uniformed employees to greet him as an important habitué, although he purchased nothing. Like an archaeologist who unearths artifacts of a civilization that has disappeared, he attended the sales to discover the objects that had been ejected from those mansions along Fifth Avenue, now demolished or put to public use. On Sundays, we often went together to the Metropolitan Museum, where the sensation of hard floors beneath my weary feet as we trudged through miles of exhibition halls, returned me to the European travels of my childhood. And as at that time, I was grateful for the nearness of my father—indefatigable even in old age—a minor Napoleon, monarch of all he surveyed.

For evenings, he had tickets for concerts, operas or theatre, and his companion was invariably a woman, no longer an actress (the breed with which he had been intimate was now gone), but she was comparatively youthful. Rosie, an exception, an old survivor from the stage, reappeared in his life as the widow of his friend, Harry Hertz. Beholden to my father, loyal and still adoring, Rosie was always on call so that he need never spend an evening alone.

One night my father, now eighty-five, my husband and I were dining at *La Côte Basque*, my father's favorite French restaurant, and he was in deep consultation with the waiter over the menu when he was interrupted by a shout. "Alfred! You haven't been taking care of yourself!"

The cry had been uttered by an old woman who stopped at our table on her way out of the restaurant. Wearing layers of floating chiffon wisps—scarf, ruffles, and capelet—she appeared to be dressed in cobwebs from the green room.

My father struggled gallantly to his feet. Although he looked unhappy, he refrained from registering any reciprocal shock.

I had not heard the introduction and after the tactless intruder had hobbled arthritically through the door, leaning on a cane and an antiquated escort, I asked who she was.

My father answered shortly, "That was Elsie Ferguson. I hardly recognized her. I didn't know she was still alive."

Elsie Ferguson's fame as an actress and a reigning beauty existed before my time, but her name was renowned. My father had never mentioned her; he still disliked talking about his affairs, which continued to reach me as fables through others. Like Ida Bright, many years earlier, this former mistress was not to mingle in family life. Even in our conversations, my father frowned upon all gossip concerning sex, saying with a dismissive wave of his padded, well-tended tan hand, "You people talk so much!"

Yet there could be no doubt about this apparition. She had mistaken the changes in my father, wrought by age, to have been caused by neglect. Time had been arrested for an instant, the present overlaid by the past, but the covering was as threadbare as a discarded stage curtain, and through the rips could be seen a celebrated relic, and an old man.

I hasten to paint my portrait of a bachelor, while the light of day still lasts.

Chapter Two

HER COUSINS AND HER UNCLES
AND HER AUNTS

Around us family life is dwindling. We are inclined to choose our relatives as we do our friends; but, just as a shopper at the market who disdains the vegetables and fruits available runs the risk of returning home to a meager meal, our discrimination may leave us isolated, deprived of the bonds of clan.

How different are the memories of my growing up, when every Sunday, with the conscientiousness of a good Catholic attending church, I visited my octogenarian grandfather. And my father's weekly family dinners—I used to groan—but now, in their absence, it is as though I had been dispossessed from a warm, crowded house whose protective walls I took for granted. Around the laden table I would be sure to find relatives of both sexes and all ages, with various genealogical claims. In accordance with custom, as quaint to contemporary ears as the Puritan addressed as "mistress" or "master," my father's guests had prefixes, "aunt," "uncle" or "cousin" attached to their names. Even friends without blood ties, who had persisted as "extras" in the wings of family life, were often dubbed with these titles, bestowed, rather than inherited.

"Aunt" Maude, as my mother's life-long friend, belonged to this genus. Following my mother's death, she became, for me, another maternal presence. Our special closeness was due, in part, to a stand maintained against forgetfulness, that secondary death inflicted by survivors upon the long deceased. Now that Maude has disappeared also, in my mind's eye I sometimes take Alma's (my mother's) place in the portrait of two young women boarding a bus for Barnard College. They are wearing trim shirtwaists and long tight skirts that must be lifted above their high-buttoned shoes as they climb the steep steps of their transportation. And when I pass my mother's girlhood home, still standing, I see the ghost of that other brown-stone across Madison Avenue, where Maude used to live, imposed like a lantern slide upon the impervious walls of an apartment building. In my imagination, I enter the phantom home and in Maude's room I discover her standing before a cheval glass, examining her reflection. As she pivots her head crowned by a coronet of chestnut curls upon her swan's throat, she counts her assets, the beauty that would earn her the worldly marriage she desires.

Years later, Aunt Maude, a veteran vamp, would complain to me with mild sarcasm, "Your mother could never learn to flirt."

Alma and Maude were actually a disparate pair: While my mother anguished over her children's chicken pox and measles, finding escape in music, her friend schemed, with the help of her husband's superior connections, to introduce her offspring at cotillions and schools where Jews were generally excluded. Outwardly they were contrasted also: Alma had classical features, her wide-set eyes were candid and thoughtful. Maude, sophisticated, resembled a minor Sarah Bernhardt in a frivolous mood, with a frizzy reddish bang, an aquiline nose and violet eyes. She dressed in costly but somewhat frayed velvet and preserved Fortuny silks, because, despite her vanity, she was incorrigibly stingy, saving pennies as diligently as she conserved the freshness of her rose-petal complexion.

My last meeting with her, at ninety-three, was in a nursing home. The frizzy bang was gone and her straight short gray locks resembled a French aristrocrat's in the tumbril on the way to the guillotine. But her eyes were still violet in her ancient, sunken face and their glance remained worldly wise, cynical, languidly humorous.

"Why haven't you been to see me?" she asked peevishly, although I had visited her only a week before. And then, confusing me with my mother, she continued ". . . too tied up at home with the children's sneezes, your books and your piano—and, of course, being the slave-wife to Alfred."

Maude had been divorced for many years. She leaned towards me, confidentially, and, back in the present, added, "Your mother was always a goose," but her voice was filled with affection.

Then, reaching into the metal institutional night table by her bed, she produced some postcards. "Look, I saved these. They're from benefit invitations, self-stamped, and I can write between the lines and mail them without it costing me a cent!"

★ ★ ★

Of "Cousin" Thelma I remember little, but the modest clearing she preempts in memory is sharply defined, like those pictures viewed through the miniature peephole in the confectioner's Easter eggs of my childhood, in which a piece of a garden or a truncated steeple appeared more vivid than an entire scene. Cousin Thelma was the estranged wife of a distant cousin of my father's. I place her in a genteel, shabby residential hotel. The living room, sunless, without individuality, was nevertheless interesting because I had heard that Thelma suffered from *sitz-platz*, a condition that made it impossible for her to venture outside into the street and forced her to remain cooped up inside her walls like a rabbit in a cage. Despite this affliction, she was uncomplaining and even respectful of her wicked husband who "kept a seamstress." For what, I wondered. He resembled a bullfrog, with inflated wattles, while Cousin Thelma was frail and pretty. She had a round child-like face, white papery skin, a delicate nose and enormous black eyes set in bruised shadows that made me think of velvety pansies that had been carelessly trampled underfoot.

Two gentlemen in my family album occupy the same page, although it is doubtful that they ever met. "Uncle" Joe, another remote cousin from the paternal branch, was homely, with large coarse features and an apologetic manner; while "Uncle" Albert, who lived in San Francisco, was handsome, like a Viennese cavalry officer. He had a white waxed moustache and clear blue eyes and he held himself erect, as though his body were encased in a corset with steel stays. The two men, the first single all his life; the second, a long-time widower who had been married to my mother's oldest sister, are paired in recall because according to the fashion for bachelors, they were lavish donors. From Uncle Joe, I received a life-sized doll, who came with a complete all-season wardrobe and, in gratitude, was named after his bestower. In my nursery he lorded over the other toys and enjoyed a superior longevity. Uncle Albert survives, chiefly, through a single episode. I am about six years old and I loiter in the foyer of our apartment which contains the magic of a player piano when he arrives, a small package in hand. The roll inside the piano is unraveling to the strains of Schubert's *Marche Militaire*, as Uncle Albert presents his gift with the flattering flourish of a courtier. I discover embedded in cotton, a fragile silver chain bracelet with sky blue links—the very color of heaven. To this day, oddly, azure enamel and the rousing music of the *Marche Militaire* remain twin seductions, while Uncle Albert is commemorated, along with a certain jeweler's box and the obsolete marvel of a mechanical piano.

"Aunt" Ella and "Uncle" Warren were not relatives at all. But, as a childless couple and old friends of my parents, my brother and I were on occasional loan to them to compensate for the vacancy in their marriage. Looking back, I realize that I disliked both of them. Aunt Ella, square, with thick legs and a pepper and salt mannish haircut, was consistently bossy. Uncle Warren was pedantic, grotesque as Beckmesser in Wagner's opera, *The Meistersingers of Nuremburg*. In memory, he appears, in all weather, wearing a dark overcoat reaching to his ankles; and Aunt

Ella is forever scolding him not to forget his scarf and rubbers, and warning him to watch his diet. They owned a townhouse in New York City and an estate in Connecticut and I experienced equal pangs of homesickness in both places. Early art patrons, Ella and Warren endowed musical events and collected Picassos from his "classical" period and poster-bright Matisse inventions, ill-assorted with the conventional decor of their rooms. They owned, also, four pampered Sealyham dogs, and although I wished that they had sufficed, I never questioned the pseudofamilial obligations expected of me. And, just as at the Thanksgiving season in my school we donated food hampers to the poor, my brother and I were deposited on the doorstep of Aunt Ella and Uncle Warren's barren residences. In later years, in return for this generosity, Aunt Ella and Uncle Warren gave lavish parties for the adolescent children of their friends.

In the long cast of relatives and so-called relatives, "Cousin" Gilda and her daughter, Mary (my age), were lead players. Gilda's father and my maternal grandfather had been cousins, and, although Leo was a prominent lawyer, for some reason he was unable to provide, adequately, for his three daughters. In addition to their fiscal disadvantages, they were so outstandingly homely that Arabella, the youngest, who in any other milieu would have been considered plain, was regarded as a beauty at home and acted as such throughout her life, according to the law of human relativity.

Gilda was short and squat, her bosom as disproportionately large as a totem object from the Easter Islands. She had a *café au lait* complexion and brown eyes that bulged with merriment. Her "arty" earrings dangled on either side of her clever parrot's face as she proclaimed, "Everyone tells me that I look like Savonarola!" Her lack of dowry and her ugliness had created for her a different history: She would probably have a long wait for a husband (if she succeeded in finding one). At a young age she dispensed charity among the impoverished Jewish immigrants of the Henry Street Settlement, becoming a special protégée of the famous social work leader, Lillian D. Wald. I now suspect that this pioneer feminist was the one great love of Gilda's life. I dredge up from my infant past a single meeting with her. Is it due to the quirkiness of memory, or might it be, simply, the physical girth of Miss Wald that has blotted out all surrounding minutiae, as well as the place and the circumstances of this encounter? I see only a monolith, resembling a Henry Moore statue. And, perhaps, because of the electric waves of worship emanating from Cousin Gilda, I felt then, and still do, that I had been in the presence of a deity. A change of occupation soon arrived for Gilda through the intervention of two fairy godmothers, a pair of millionaire sisters, also devotees of Miss Wald, who provided funds for a neighborhood theatre, which, in time, became *The Henry Street School*. Situated uptown, classless, it provided a superior education in the performing arts, hatching many successful examples; it flourishes to this day. Eventually Gilda, with no previous training, through her friendships and her natural audacity and verve, became its president for the duration of her days. And, just as Jean-Jacques Rousseau, the eighteenth-century intellectual, was known for his glorification of the "noble savage," Gilda, born and bred a bourgeois, identified with bohemians: the actors, dancers and directors of the school who inspired her with unswerving allegiance.

Gilda was a chronic namedropper: "So I said to Kit . . .", "Greg consults me about everything . . ." "Martha is a stunning human . . ."

And we all knew that she was referring to Katherine Cornell, Gregory Peck and Martha Graham.

Gilda's marriage had lasted just long enough to engender Mary, a quiet girl, fair, rosy-cheeked, blue-eyed and buxom; to others, she might appear ordinary, but to her mother she was a creature of almost miraculous perfection. At moments, it seemed that Gilda could hardly give credence to having produced this paragon. And just as in some forms of insect life, the male species, having justified its existence by the fertilization of the female, dies, Gilda's husband was forgotten or recalled only in jest.

"I never understood why Maurice took it so amiss that I was obliged to laugh at the 'act' on our wedding night."

The precise meaning of the words had evaded me, but I sensed the shocked censure of the adults present.

During the winter months, I walked the few blocks separating our apartment from Gilda's to "play" with Mary. Although their home was small, dark and cramped, my mother always openly admired Gilda's talent for interior decoration. The living room was ornamented with contemporary objets d'art, among them I recall a terra-cotta sculpture of two elongated heads pressed close together, a mother and child. Although they were almost featureless, Gilda's appreciation had persuaded me that the statue expressed Tenderness in its most sublime form. A china rooster on the mantel was distinguished because it was a gift from Mabel Dodge Luhan out of her adobe house in Taos that she shared with Tony, her husband, a full-blooded American Indian. Unlike our dining room table covered with a white cloth, Gilda used coarse straw mats and, in place of florist flowers and silver candlesticks, her center-piece was a pottery bowl sprouting dried sheaves of wheat.

But the most interesting spot in the apartment was Mary's room, with its suite of royal blue furniture. The door of the wooden wardrobe depicted the Virgin, full length, complete with the spikes of radiant halo and the "babe" in arms, garlanded with field flowers and small, primitive animal forms, the latter motifs repeated on the bed's head and footboards and ladder-backed chairs. It never occurred to Mary or me that this decor might be unsuitable to a Jewish city child. But it did not seem to quite belong to Mary, either; rather, it was a stage set—*inside a Bavarian chalet*, in which Gilda placed her daughter, also a "stunning person," a miscast leading lady.

Visits "backstage" were privileges bestowed upon Mary and me. After the magic of the play or dance recital, at the curtain's fall, the embarrassing moment never failed to arrive. Although I hung back modestly, claiming that Mary, as daughter, should go without me, Cousin Gilda was impervious to my protests. "Rubbish! Kit (Martha, Doris or Ruth) just love having you there!"

And, an engine in the lead, she dragged us through dark, sooty corridors along iron stairs to the dressing room that smelled of greasepaint belonging to the star. We would find this person in perspiration, exhausted from the effort of the performance, removing false eyelashes, wig and makeup, besieged by fellow artists clamorous with articulate congratulations. Cousin Gilda, undaunted, pushed us forward until we stood mute, before the star who appeared disappointing without the remove of the stage and the benefit of footlights. And just as a ventriloquist speaks through his dummy, Gilda gave voice to our admiration, and we were permitted to escape.

Now, when anyone suggests going backstage after a concert or play, my refusal is as automatic as reflex. I feel myself a school girl again in the company of Mary and Cousin Gilda. I smell greasepaint and shrink from confronting the performer, as though I were being asked to congratulate a new mother not yet out of the delivery room.

At this time, years after Gilda's death, in the attempt to disinter my memories of her, I am, arbitrarily, confronted with the surreal sight of two hollow pillars. They flank the door of a rented house in Westchester County, which, unlike its English-Georgian or American-Colonial neighbors, is an imitation Petit Trianon. But it was outstanding, especially because of the discrepancy between its front and back. Due to the miserliness of the owner, the façade, fronting the road, was refurbished the color of strawberries, to suggest pink marble, while the rear, hidden from motorists, was prison gray, with paint peeling and flaking, falling upon the dandelion-studded grass like snow, soiled and unseasonable. The interior was sparsely furnished; the rooms, large and drafty, inadequately equipped. My mother reproached herself for having made a bad choice. But Gilda exclaimed, "What fun! It's like an indoor picnic!"

On the rolling lawn, I spot four people: A thunderstorm is brewing, the sky frowns, gun-metal dark, and the wind catches up the flimsy wicker garden furniture, scattering it in all directions like dead leaves. My mother, Mary and I stumble after the flying chairs, chaise longues and tables, always out of reach, while Gilda, on the sidelines, observes the performance enthusiastically, her brown eyes popping at the fun, her "arty" earrings swinging on either side of her clever parrot's face.

London's Hotel Connaught stands for that city as much as Westminster Abbey, Trafalgar Square or an indigenous crescent or mews. An oversized doorman attends the entrance, rigidly dignified in scarlet, gold-braided uniform, more resplendent even than the Palace guards in their shakos. The lobby is dark, glossy with well-polished wood; the furniture, traditional. The atmosphere resembles a club, the restless arrivals and departures of ordinary hotels has, somehow, been subdued to a minimum and while the welcome by the concierge is cool and correct, he seems to be reassuring the clientele that they "belong," that a stay at the Connaught, though dear, is not a mere commercial transaction.

Adjacent to the lobby is a small sitting room where every afternoon a British tea is served, accompanied by scones and paper-thin watercress sandwiches presented on flowered porcelain and accompanied by the hum of polite conversation. Several years ago, while I was waiting to meet a friend in the lobby of the Connaught, the sound of hilarious laughter issuing from the tea salon broke the habitual hush. Looking inside, I was surprised by the sight of Cousin Gilda, now in her eighties, enthroned upon a Chippendale chair, while at her feet, like worshippers before an icon, a group of very young men, obviously aspiring actors, crouched upon the floor. I had not seen cousin Gilda or Mary for years: Time and altered mores had moved me, unwittingly, away from the extended family enclaves of my youth. Mary and I had never had much in common, our intimacy was based on propinquity, and, without the presence of my mother, Gilda's bubbling vivacity seemed more irritatingly affected than high-spirited. Now engrossed in holding court, she had not noticed me standing in the opening to the salon. Should I interrupt her act? A wave of nostalgia engulfed me—not for Mary, now securely married to a banker and living in the suburbs with four children; she had not, after all, taken to the life of Art her mother had envisioned for her. Nor for Gilda, herself, who would greet me, after all this time, with scant enthusiasm, and introduce me to the acolytes with that well-remembered, self-satisfied sniff through her long nose. I hesitated on the threshold, held back by feelings undefinable and conflicted.

"You must come to New York," Gilda was saying to her rapt listeners, "I will introduce you to Sandy. He is a stunning person, a divine director. To work with him is a rich experience."

Despite her age, Gilda had not changed, not even in appearance, the Easter Island totem silhouette was the same, her brown eyes still bulged with artistic appreciation, only the dangling hoop earrings were missing; the piano stood, but the metronome had been removed. The slowing of the tempo would go unmeasured; old age was not for Gilda any more than a life of business in London's City was meant for the young actors of her entourage.

". . . we are all artists . . ." I imagined hearing her say with that rehearsed British accent, in well-placed projection of voice that could be heard in the last row of the balcony.

I turned away, and I never saw Cousin Gilda again, nor even thought of her until now.

Chapter Three

THE FRIEND OF BRAHMS

When my family moved from the apartment where I had been born a few blocks north in New York City, we left behind the "music room." I never saw, again, the magical player piano whose keys jumped up and down without benefit of human hands, while rolls of perforated paper brought forth a repertory of rousing notes; the phonograph, cranked like a Model T Ford with a horn in the shape of a giant morning glory had also vanished. In the music room I often examined the oil painting of my mother's sister, Bessie, deceased shortly after she posed for it: a solemn four-year-old holding an unnaturally middle-aged–looking wooden doll on her beruffled lap. I don't know why this melancholy portrait graced the music room, but it is embalmed in memory in all its details, from the child's artificially frizzed fair hair to her polished black boots demurely crossed beneath the hem of her elaborately adult dress.

I was relieved when Bessie disappeared. The bust of Beethoven, in somber silhouette against the window went with her. In which secondhand Hall of Fame might it be located now? It presided over our music room, immovable, with fierce bronze features, deep eye sockets beneath shaggy brows and tousled locks petrified into perpetuity, as though the Master emerging from a storm had found shelter but no thaw in our cluttered music room. The bust was cold to the touch, and it rested on a columnar pedestal, white as a marble headstone.

Only the Steinway piano followed us to our new home. For the bust of Beethoven, the living presence of Madam Marguereta Dessoff, founder and director of the Dessoff Choir, was substituted. To my childish view she appeared as ponderous as the bust of Beethoven and almost as famous. For it was said that in the "old country," Madam Dessoff had been the friend of Brahms. How ancient she must be! And why had she descended from such Olympian heights to our apartment, which contained only a conventional piano and my mother, an undistinguished member of the choir who often apologized for the meagerness of her voice and talent.

Since Madam Dessoff's arrival in the United States predated Hitler, I know, in retrospect, that she was not a refugee, but according to the romantic historical novels I had read, she did not fit the *emigré* category, either. She was no swashbuckler and there wasn't an aristocratic *von* attached to her name. I also realized that immigrants did not issue straight from Ellis Island up to the podium at Town Hall. So Marguereta Dessoff was an unclassified foreigner; but alien she remained and, as such, an object of curiosity to me. Despite the honorific appellative of "Madam," she was a spinster like my governesses and like them, she had a heavy German accent that sounded reprimanding even when she was attempting to be gracious. She had a long equine face, large bony nose and small watery blue eyes. Her forehead was always a suffused red, due, I imagined, to the heat of inspiration, or, perhaps, because of some inner self-contained anger. Her thinning white hair was pinned into a scanty bun and her body was as stiff and flat as an ironing board. And just like the women I had observed along the less fashionable side streets of the Left Bank in Paris, dressed in perpetual mourning, carrying loaves of bread, like fish in shopping nets, Madam Dessoff always wore black and held a briefcase filled with sheet music—her work. Enthusiastically shared with my mother, it excluded me, and I resented Madam Dessoff's intrusion into our home. In winter, I daydreamed that she might slip on the icy pavement and impair her baton-wielding right arm. Or, better, I hoped that some heretofore unknown rich relative might die, leaving her a fortune, and that Madam Dessoff would retire to Germany forever. None of this came to pass. And I can no longer recall just when she drifted from my particular notice and I grew indifferent to her hold on my mother, her foreignness and her eccentric way of life. In time, even the tag "Friend of Brahms," lost its power, too, becoming no more than an expired passport, the debris of forgotten travels.

The rehearsals of the Dessoff Choir were hours of liberation for my mother. I used to watch her as she left home; I see again the olive green wool dress she often wore with the string of long amber beads, a single concession to ornamentation. But the effect of the necklace was less decorative than constricting, like a leash or a self-imposed

noose. As she waited for the elevator to arrive, a Cinder-
ella's coach to take her off, my mother, usually too familiar
for notice, was altered before my eyes into another: a young
girl, a stranger in the house.

At Carnegie Hall, two places in the orchestra are
now occupied by ghosts: my former self and the shadowy
presence of my long-dead mother. But, I cannot reconstruct
that physical person seated beside me; I see only two
delicate hands with tapered fingers clasped, as in prayer, on
top of a business-like leather bag. And I remember a
daughter's withdrawal, her deliberate resistance to the
seduction of music—her mother's domain. She refuses to
share the other's joy. Side by side, they are separated by the
daughter's assertion of feigned deafness.

If my response to music at other times was throttled,
at the performance of the Dessoff Choir, resistance swelled
to hostility. When the a cappella chorus trooped on stage, I
spotted my mother immediately in the midst of the motley
crowd of men and women. She appeared embarrassingly
familiar, her face indecently exposed. As in a graduation
photograph, the choir lined up, row upon row. There she
was in the back, towards the right, still conspicuous! Madam
Dessoff mounted the podium. She raised her baton and her
authority increased, becoming almost male. I seemed to
detect the outlines of a tailcoat, an aura of distinction,
surrounding her severe black dress. The choir erupted,
losing its variousness, it grew into one multi-voiced instrument soaring up to the Savior in praise and supplication.
Now my mother was remote, but I could still distinguish
her dwindled face, a small white disk in the general mosaic.
The voices mounted to Heaven, the entire chorus seemed

to rise, they were the angels on the high, vaulted ceiling of a European cathedral—beyond reach, infinitely distanced, obscured by drapery clouds of melody. Only the leader held her place, solidly planted on her platform. Yet it was she who had caused the unearthly flight, she was the mannish magician who had wafted my mother away with a wave of her magic stick, transforming her into a creature more unsubstantial than flesh and blood, the barely visible, expressionless face in the moon. At those times, my curiosity concerning Marguereta Dessoff grew into passionate dislike.

In summer, the Dessoff Choir disbanded. Sometimes we spent the vacation on Saranac Lake, where my parents rented Pine Brook Camp, modestly named, since it consisted of a colony of pseudo-rustic log buildings, large and numerous enough to welcome a population of house guests, including many single women (friends of my mother's), with no place of their own. Madam Dessoff was, of course, among them. In memory, I am able to skip again along the narrow boardwalk connecting the houses—the sleeping quarters (children and adults separate), Grandfather's bungalow, the dining hall, the servant's accommodations, the "rumpus room" above the boat house. And, just as an exile harbors within him his natal village no matter how far off it may be, I, too, am able to recreate in detail the geography of Pine Brook Camp and those Adirondack summers despite the distance of years. I recall the excursions; setting out in canoe, rowboat or motor launch to picnic on one of the islands dotting the lake, or to visit, by water route, neighbors in similar "rustic" establishments. I hear the splashing of water against the shore, the dipping of oars and the spluttering of engines that left rainbow trails of gasoline. At night, one could catch the hoot of an owl in the encroaching woods. The camp was a cheerful, artificial clearing in the dense tenebrous forest that still held nature's secrets inviolate. There, mushrooms, toadstools and fungi proliferated. We etched out initials, entwined, and hearts and arrows, in the pallid, spongy surfaces of the fungi that clung like goiters to the rough bark of the trees. When summer ended we returned to the city with souvenirs: Indian moccasins, feathered headdresses and pillows stuffed with aromatic pine needles, their cases stamped with pictures of the lake. But, although it crumbled, I preserved, for as long as possible, a rotting fungus. More than anything else, its aroma stood for remembrance; a Valentine nostalgic with a past love: Saranac Lake in summertime.

At Pine Brook Camp we never sat down to meals fewer than fourteen at table. We had assigned places at the long board beneath the glassy stare of a stuffed moose hanging over the fireplace. My grandfather was seated at the head, flanked by Sofia, his companion, with Marguereta Dessoff at his other side, because she was able to converse with him in his native German. I listened to her foreign words with distaste, yet I liked to hear my grandfather speaking German, proud of his bilingual skills. It was embarrassing to watch Madam Dessoff as she exerted herself to amuse my taciturn relative; just as a mother coaxes a baby with tempting morsels, she fed him anecdote after anecdote. But he never responded, continuing to eat in sullen silence, his white napkin tucked beneath his snowy beard. Where was that other Madam Dessoff, the commanding personage on the podium, the aggressive intruder into our city apartment, carrying her bag of musical notes? Was it possible that she was this supplicant, homeless guest trying patiently to earn our hospitality?

"Herr Liebmann, I must tell you a little story . . ."

This was even worse than the other self: this outsider who grovelled and attempted, in vain, to ingratiate herself, to fit, even, while remaining conspicuously different from the rest of us.

Ignited by my present disgust combined with former resentments and abetted by the cooperation of Mary, my cousin, I plotted the downfall of Marguereta Dessoff. After lunch, at rest hour, lying on our army cots on the sleeping porch fragrant with the surrounding pines, while sucking lollipops, we hatched our plan. When it was completed, we approached the enemy, demanding a meeting at the boat house, the site of important events at Pine Brook Camp. The "rumpus room" commanded the most scenic view of the Lake. Furnished in birch bark, with Indian rugs and cushions, it was here that we performed plays, held Ping-Pong tournaments, birthday and Fourth of July entertainments, and music recitals. But the piano was too out of tune, mildewed from dampness, to be used by Madam Dessoff.

It was on the ground floor of the boat house, surrounded, but not concealed by canoes and rowboats that I had seen my first naked man. A weekend visitor fresh from a dip in the lake, he stood, bath towel in hand, lazily drying his exposed body, unaware of my peeping eyes. I was fascinated by what looked like a heavy black mustache (contrasting with his city-white flesh), flourishing around his genitals. It was at the boat house, too, that I rested from my initial triumphant long swim in water over my head, and it was to this portentous place that we summoned Marguereta Dessoff.

Surprisingly, she agreed to meet us at the appointed hour. It was odd how eager she was to be friendly, when in the city she took no notice of me. Like a deposed monarch, without her music, Madam Dessoff was divested of power. The contract that Mary and I had drawn up—did we really believe in it? Madam Dessoff placed her wire-rimmed spectacles on her bony nose and read with care. We had challenged her to a game of croquet! If she lost, she was to enter the lake, without a life preserver or any other aid, and, as she feared water and did not know how to swim, we were pretty certain that she would drown. I no longer remember our forfeit were she to win—*she could not win.* Mary had suggested her signing in blood, but the idea made me queasy and we settled for ordinary ink. Madam Dessoff affixed her name to the paper, ours, beneath hers. Even her penmanship was old-fashioned, foreign, small, pointed, gothic, the letters uniformly regular as those on an old scroll, while we wrote the large round "manuscript" printing taught at our progressive schools.

We told only Cousin Gilda about the plan, swearing her to secrecy, counting on her sense of the dramatic to go along with the event, and we appointed her referee. The morning of the contest dawned fine, the brilliant sunshine still too pristine to temper the nip in the air. The croquet lawn was studded with dew, the terrain would be slow. At either end of the field, wooden stakes painted in multi-colored horizontal stripes, were hammered into the ground. Just as jousting knights brandish their poles, the sight of the croquet stakes fixed at their places, start and finish, spurred us to battle. Madam Dessoff arrived, dressed as usual, in neat, prim black. Did I expect to see her in the tatters of a condemned criminal? We all aimed for the stake. The enemy hit it squarely, with a professional thud. She would have the advantage of starting after us—a bad beginning. Mary and I, taking turns, would have to work all the harder. The balls rolled in slow motion through the wire wickets, small hoops planted in the drenched grass like miniature arches of triumph. We took aim, knocking the enemy as far from her course as rules permitted. Armies, in opposition, we advanced upon one another.

Gilda stood on the sidelines, her long earrings jiggling emphatically as she called errors. But in the pretend log cabins everyone still slept, innocent of war raging not far away!

Despite the cool morning, I was sweating and had to stop often to wipe the perspiration from my eyes and forehead. Madam Dessoff took aim, she held her mallet at its base at a peculiar angle, like an outdated underhand tennis service. She must have learned croquet at some German spa long ago. Over the grass, the balls rolled—the red and the blue—first one in the lead, then the other, closely matched. The final goal was now near; my heart pounded so hard I felt it might burst through my middy blouse. I held my breath. My grievances against Madam Dessoff were no longer clear—winning was all. Time stood still, my vision narrowed. Now I saw only the stake with its barber-pole stripes grown tall as a tower. Thud! My red ball hit its side. Dizzy and unbelieving, I stood up straight: I was the victor.

We filed down to the dock for the funeral ceremony. Madam Dessoff began by removing her shoes. I thought that, perhaps, she should have worn them into the water as weights, but then I remembered that she could not swim anyway. Next, she started to tug a ring over a knuckle, large and knobby with arthritis. It was a heavy gold signet with a masculine-looking onyx seal. I wondered if her friend, Brahms, had once used it as a watch fob on a chain spanning his dignified girth. She handed it to Gilda who responded with a moving oration about treasuring the gift, always, in memory of her illustrious fellow guest and their last summer together in the beautiful Adirondack Mountains. Her prominent brown eyes sparkled but her words were appropriately mournful.

Madam Dessoff walked towards the ladder and the dark waiting water. Suddenly, I noticed a small frog wriggling against the steps in a vain attempt to reach land. I had an impulse to rescue the poor, helpless, slippery little creature, to place it in the dry safety of my palm, but I restrained myself. Madam Dessoff grasped the sides of the ladder, her back towards the lake. She seemed to be saying goodbye to her orphaned orthopedic shoes that looked somehow pathetic, toeing in slightly, abandoned on the sun-warmed boards of the dock. Madam Dessoff slowly descended the first rung of the ladder. Mary and I, beside ourselves with excitement, were jumping up and down, urging her further. All at once a command, sharp as a shot, rang out.

"Stop at once! Gilda, how could you . . . ? Marguereta, I apologize! These foolish girls shall be punished for their idiotic, unforgivable behavior."

Was this my gentle mother who disliked giving orders and had never been a disciplinarian?

Cousin Gilda looked ill at ease, the most uncomfortable of amateur actresses. She returned the ring without flourish to Madam Dessoff who was calmly, methodically, reknotting her shoelaces.

Mary and I were left alone, deflated. The strenuous contest was voided. What had we intended? How far could we go? Madam Dessoff and Gilda—to them the whole thing had been a joke. I smarted at the perfidy of grownups towards children.

When Marguereta Dessoff died, she willed my mother a pair of brocaded satin Louis XV chairs brought from her home in Germany. For years they stood in my family's living room, two frivolous outsiders among our heavy, solemn English reproductions. Unrepresentative, also, of their Teutonic donor, the chairs looked like French lap dogs who had strayed into a pack of Anglo-Saxon hounds. Coquettish, with spindly, bowed legs, they always remained conspicuous and outmoded and were referred to as "Madam Dessoff's chairs" long after the old chorus director (my mother having died, too) had been forgotten.

On winter afternoons I like to walk around the reservoir in Central Park. The air crackles with cold. To the south, towers cut their sharp edges into a curds-and-whey sky. Gulls and ducks gather in separate gray and white clusters on the frozen water slashed by incisions of light. Everywhere, color has been replaced by definition. On the path behind me and ahead, the feet of joggers, breathing hard, thud along their alloted track. Yet a gentler sound prevails: the soft lapping of the wavelets against the side of the reservoir where tall weeds, blanched as winter wheat, wave their tasselled heads in the arctic wind. I press my face against the enclosing wire fence: a prisoner barred from a secret out there upon the water. The insinuating murmur grows insistent; it is a summer voice and I am engulfed by sound. I no longer feel the bite of January's cold, or notice the ragged bulrushes and squatting birds. I am listening to the waves licking the shore in perpetual caress. In my mind's eye a different scene comes into focus, imposing itself upon the so-called present: an idyllic vacation lake dotted with green islands. Small waves splash against a sun-blistered dock on which two children in pink and blue middy blouses and bloomers are jumping. Mad whirling dervishes, they circle a motionless figure, a petrified, neolithic species. And just as clouds scurry on (destination unknown), uncovering patches of clear sky, through a rift in time the magic tricks of mnemonics conjure up a series of pictures long buried in the subconscious. The past is not dead, it only hides in unsuspected places.

Chapter Four

HOMAGE TO THE STEAM LOCOMOTIVE

It is not my nature to wax sentimental about the past. I do not see my childhood as an exceptionally happy state and, furthermore, it no longer seems to be mine. Even the beloved dead, in time, relax their hold upon memory, but occasionally, a place or an object will come out of hiding and like a person, drowning, I will grasp it, a life preserver, in a sea of forgetfulness.

One hot summer's day, I sat, absorbed by the glossy pages of a fashion magazine, in the air-conditioned deep-freeze of an electric Amtrak commuters' train. After leaving Grand Central Station, we fled the shocking, pitiful decayed countenances—broken window panes, like missing teeth, of Harlem's house fronts—into the pseudo-countryside of the suburbs, intercepted by an arterial system of thruways. The clickety-clack clickety-clack of wheels on rails was saying something to me: laying aside the magazine, I gave my whole attention to that voice, but its message evaded me. *Clickety-clack, clickety-clack.* Gradually a single strain detached itself from the general cacophony and, like the haunting refrain of a piano in a concerto that soars above the combined sounds of a symphony orchestra, the insinuating notes nudged me backward.

A child, I found myself installed in a snug nest of a compartment on a French train en route with my family from Cherbourg to Paris. It was the summer vacation season and our little band occupied the whole space. Facing one another, on the plush antimacassared sofas were: my mother, father, Bini, the French maid, Mademoiselle, and a transient tutor who remains featureless as a wax dummy in a department store. I strain to return the others, but they are here only in instants, on the wings of a random word or gesture, moths drawn to a flickering light bulb. But, in the string hammocks above our head, I see, distinctly, our hats, old-fashioned as museum pieces. If I had been clairvoyant, my mother's black straw would have been an omen of her untimely death, not so many years off. Bini's headgear is similar, perhaps it is a hand-me-down, rendered cheerful by a bright blue ribbon cockade retrieved from her sewing basket where every scrap is conserved; my father's white Panama is banded by a Sulka foulard tie; my brother's visored cap, an odd period piece, as is my bonnet trimmed with artificial daisies and cherries. These obsolete articles of dress are stand-ins for the leading players on tour in Europe. For me, the compartment was home, a recurrent hyphen between foreign city and foreign city. Its decor, invariable, greeted us with the same photographs of famous sites, and signs warned us in four languages that it was dangerous to lean out of the windows. I hear the echo of my mother's caveat, directed at my brother and me, not to venture out into the hall beyond our warm cocoon, for fear of drafts that might lurk there. Soon a gong resounded down the aisle and a voice announced the first luncheon service. My father in the lead, we marched along the train, car after car, balancing precariously, at the jiggling agitated joinings. No food has ever tasted as delicious as the *potage* of vegetables that opened the meal. And the gleaming white china with the company's trademark **W** (wagon-lits) emblazoned in gold, in my view, was fit for kings. After endless courses, the meal was concluded by its signature of assorted cheeses and fruits, but even when I could eat no more, I remained hungry for the sight of the French farmland scurrying past the dining car windows—every inch of space cultivated, nothing wasted. Neat patchworks of vineyards embroidered the hills, and haystacks dotted the fields above a red and blue carpet of poppies and cornflowers. Farmers paused, briefly, in their labor to watch our transit, and children holding bouquets of wild flowers waved up at us, and I waved back as we sped by. With a shriek of wicked glee, the locomotive plunged us into a tunnel, and when we emerged into sunlight again, the whistle took on a different tune, gentler, as though the engine has been sated through the performance of its power. Ahead at a bend in the track, I could see the locomotive, its smokestack ejecting steam, and a delicate trail wafted in our direction, the white feather of peace proffered by the victor to the vanquished.

No matter how much I resented days spent in foreign cities and longed to be home in the company of my friends, I was always sorry to leave the somewhat shabby splendor of our hotel accommodations. No sooner had I managed to carve a sheltering nook in some strange bedroom, embellished by a giant wardrobe, worn velvet armchairs, a marble bust of Marie-Antoinette and damask drapes, which were not capable of muffling the unfriendly night noises of an alien town outside the tall windows—the shrill of taxi horns, the striking of hours in a clock tower unnoticed during the day—then we would be off again and the process would start anew. At departure, our valises waited, packed and locked, and the steamer trunks (half closet, half bureau) stood at readiness for the arrival of the hotel porter. Sitting in my temporary home about to be vacated, rendered melancholy through the imminence of abandonment, I would cling to the furry comfort of a teddy bear (later, I drugged myself on the pages of a Tauchnitz edition novel).

One day on a walk along the Rue de Rivoli, I spotted in the showcase of a trinket store a statuette of a ballet dancer. Her tutu was made of brittle porcelain net, her feet shod in pink slippers, a wreath of embossed flowers encircled her neat head. The object was so alluring that I determined it should be mine. When my father presented me with a package, I found the figurine pillowed inside, bedded in layers of tissue paper. On this occasion, leave taking went unnoticed as I examined my treasured amulet. I no longer recall when the accident occurred and the statuette was found broken at the bottom of a staircase, the perky china tutu chipped in several places, one slender leg severed from the body. Futile attempts were made to paste the lost limb, but the dancer ended her existence in a Berlin hotel scrap basket. I hardly grieved at her demise, the talisman having by then lost its magic.

I am persuaded that the asphalt of a venerable train station bears the invisible imprints of thousands of shoes.

Although the members of our family tourist group are long dead, and I, the only survivor no longer recognize myself in a child holding a toy bear, I feel that we have left fragments of ourselves embedded like mica dust along the routes to the trains. For me, the station was the heartbeat of travel; destination a lesser thing than movement. And just as in grand opera an extra may experience a sense of exhilaration and rejoice at the proximity of the "stars," I relished the sight of an Indian rajah, a renowned heiress or a matinee idol marching in step with me, sharing the smoky yellow light slanting down from the vaulted glass roof criss-crossed by iron girders. Though I savored these dramatic moments, I was curious, also, about American girls of my own age; coinciding briefly on the platform, we eyed one another like dogs on leashes, sniffing and straining towards their own kind.

I think of those long-ago European travels when I find myself in an airport: antiseptic, synthetic, commercial, resembling a shopping mall, not synonymous with adventure. The multilingual voices issuing from the loudspeaker system seem to blend in a single lingua franca, the place of disembarkation will be identical territory of tacky store displays, rubberized floors, plastic accoutrements with the same bored voice announcing arrivals and departures. And the plane—that mechanical bird capable of carrying its passengers to the ends of the earth in no time at all—hides, unassumingly, beyond a makeshift covered walk. And, just as a sleeper who wakes each morning takes for granted the quotidian miracle of the transition from dream to reality, we step inside a plane, oblivious to the little understood wonders of flight.

How other was the steam locomotive! My entrails vibrated as it roared into view; the engineer perched aloft in his cab was dwarfed. The train appeared propelled by its own sweating strength, every oiled part working in unison, as it came to a panting halt beside me. Once the pride of the Industrial Revolution, the steam locomotive has now dwindled into legend . . . in the far-off days, before the Second World War, there lived an archaic beast whose palace was the great, lofty cave of the railroad station. . . .

At night, the compartment of the wagon-lit was even snugger and the clickety-clack of the wheels louder; sound taking over from sight as the train devoured the shrouded countryside. Sitting bolt upright, my father snored, but when we stopped at a wayside station, he awoke immediately and jumped out. Upon his return, he provided us with sandwiches, hard, crisp rolls with ham, like tender pink cat tongues. Sometimes he lingered so long outside that he had to be hoisted back onto the train when it was already in motion. We greeted him as a hero, but I prayed that he would take no more risks lest we be abandoned, orphan children, in a foreign land at night! *Clickety-clack, clickety-clack*, the cars were rolling again and the insistent clatter became a song. In adolescence I would bestow upon it a popular tune of the day, "Who stole my heart away, who makes me dream all day . . . ?" I had no answer to the question but I pressed myself against the window as though I might discern out there the non-existent form of an unknown lover. In the lighted compartment, the glass showed me my own features reflected in an onyx mirror.

★ ★ ★

Last winter in Paris, I visited the Quai d'Orsay Museum of Art. For years, the landmark railroad station was shut down, the building having outlived its use. Briefly, Orson Welles had preempted the space as a location for a film, and then workmen invaded it to gut the interior and transform it into a gallery. In the chill drizzle, I stood in a long line waiting to enter, eager to bathe again in the smoky, golden mist filtering through the giant skylight criss-crossed by iron beams. The crowd was inching its way forward, coughing and sneezing, and I stamped my frozen feet in a vain effort to keep warm. A helpful woman standing nearby advised me to break rank and to slip into position further ahead, "I have done it several times myself," she encouraged me. Feeling like a robber, I moved furtively nearer to my goal, urged on by the promise of loot, the recapturing of the old depot with its rich horde of memories. I avoided eyes, thinking I might encounter suspicion of my transgression in their glances, but there were no reproaches and, at last, from my purloined situation, I stepped inside.

Although I consider myself a seasoned traveler, I have never learned the tourist's primary lesson, that a sight eagerly anticipated often proves disappointing. It is the unexpected that arrests: a flock of clouds over the Luxembourg Gardens, or a glimpse of a cobbled courtyard through a grill gate on a narrow medieval street on the Left Bank may leave more impression than the bulk of Nôtre Dame or the harmonious architecture of the Place des Vosges. Now, at last, I found myself under the lofty glass roof, but the mysterious, sooty yellow light had been scrubbed into the clarity required for an exhibition hall. As in a nightmare in which one is lost in the familiar, I tried to find my way back to the station, to retrace my footsteps to the platforms where the trains used to rush upon me. But there were no shining cars, no tracks, nor porters in blue smocks, and the purposeful migration of the crowds had been replaced by the leisurely amble of visitors in a gallery, their voices hushed as worshippers in a church. And the steam locomotives? The well-intentioned memorial had buried them in depth.

I left abruptly. Outside, the black winter rain was still falling and as I looked back I saw the Gare Quai d'Orsay, an empty conch shell whose vital insides had been eroded by time and progress.

Chapter Five

FAMILY DOCTOR

In my family, death was unmentionable before children, yet illness, its covert harbinger, was never far away. We had no God to fortify us, as religion, in any form, was outlawed by my militantly atheist father. Although my parent seemed immune to any morbid uncertainties concerning the mysteries of the universe and the fragile hold of humans upon it, I, while admiring and envying his stalwart earthiness, was unable to follow him. At night, in the dark before sleep, I would be seized by metaphysical jim-jams and a familiar litany would buzz through my head: *Who am I? I might have been a rock, a toad, a blade of grass* . . . In those days, I was as preoccupied by the void prior to birth as by death, its more generally feared counterpart. With the intuition of childhood, I sensed their alikeness, their equally horrifying state of non-being.

We did not, however, navigate without help. There was the family physician, and our belief in the powers of Leopold Stieglitz remained a constant for all the forty-odd years that he attended us. At that period for Jews, assimilated, agnostic, bourgeois, the doctor could assume priestly capacities. He was our bulwark; and just as sailors lost at sea offer prayers of thankfulness at the sight of land, the patient and the anxious relatives breathed fervent sighs of relief when Dr. Stieglitz appeared, framed in the bedroom door.

He was a compact figure, dressed, invariably, in neat clerical black, with a starched white shirt collar. He had firm, healthy, rosy skin, jet eyes, at once bright and profound, a generous, aquiline, authoritative nose, a bald, domed forehead and, as long as I knew him, he wore a small goatee, like a blob of white sterile cotton, upon his chin. An early portrait showed a resemblance to the young Dr. Sigmund Freud: Then, the polished pate had been thatched with dark hair and he sported a flourishing beaver beard; he posed, head in hand, and his black eyes gazed out with brooding, romantic melancholy. As with all leaders, myths collected around Dr. Stieglitz, worldly rather than spiritual. He had received his medical education before the First World War, in Heidelberg, in the company of Julius, his identical twin. Although I hardly knew this sibling (having seen him only once or twice when I ran into him on the street where I mistook him for the doctor), he had a certain fascination due to his linkage to Leopold. "In Chicago, when Julius has a twinge of gout in his toe, I experience, simultaneously, the same pain," the doctor used to relate, and this physical phenomenon became legend. In Heidelberg, the brothers met two German sisters, and I pictured the foursome seated in a field of wild flowers with the crenellated towers of a medieval Teutonic castle in the background. Before returning to America, they pledged their troths and, their careers established—one a doctor in

New York City, the other a chemist in Chicago—they sent for the *gretchens*, but not before Leopold's eyes had alighted upon my father's sister, Amanda, at a bowling club, and he had fallen helplessly in love at first sight. A proper Victorian gentleman, he would keep his word and marry the housewifely *fraulein*, while smoldering, morosely for my dumpy, sallow, imperious aunt. In our circle it was told that despite their marriages the romantic affair between Amanda and Leopold, endured, on and off, throughout their lives.

When the doctor sat at the edge of my sickbed, counting my pulse beats on his old-fashioned, heavy, gold pocket watch, my feverish wrist held in his competent, cool hand, he would sometimes remark, "You remind me of your aunt . . ."

And then the grippe or chicken pox became almost pleasurable because I identified with a heightened love story—like a diminished Camille—seen through the wrong end of the telescope.

Although Amanda might have been his harem queen, rumors about the doctor's reputation as a womanizer reached my ears as I grew up, and I viewed with suspicion his photographic image upon the dressing tables of female patients. But nothing could disturb for the "faithful" their reliance on his supernatural gift for healing.

In retrospect, first meetings have elegiac import unsuspected at the moment of their occurrence. I now see in small detail the doctor's entrance into my life. It is difficult to believe, today, when surgical procedures take place in impersonal operating theatres, in hospitals, that my brother and I underwent tonsillectomies in the cozy familiarity of our nursery. Although the coming event had been kept secret from us, on the appointed morning our nursery had suddenly been transformed into a chill lunar landscape, with white sheets padding the walls and shrouding the furniture. The juvenile pictures, illustrations from *Red Riding Hood, Peter, Pumpkin Eater* (framed behind unshatterable isinglass), were blotted out, and chairs and bureaus resembled snowy mountain forms. I can no longer distinguish the person of the surgeon, and the accompanying anesthesiologist; I remember, only faintly, my terror at the ether cone placed over my nose and mouth, the sweetish heavy fumes and the concentric colored circles before my eyes as I struggled for breath. The pain and gore are forgotten, also. I awoke from oblivion to see two ripe black cherry eyes shining above a surgical mask: Dr. Stieglitz had been called in by my parents because they did not trust the merely physical expertise of the surgeon, and my pediatrician, inadequate, too, had been banished. Like a first communicant, wearing a sterile shower cap in place of wreath and veil, all unknowingly, I was inducted into the cult of doctor worshippers.

From a seeming distance, a voice ordered, "As soon as she can keep it down, give her small sips of ice-cold milk."

It had been forbidden by the deposed pediatrician who thought that I was allergic. And, now, a lifetime later, at the taste of that bland product, a lunar nursery, a lost ambrosia potion and my introduction to Dr. Leopold Stieglitz are made present.

Every religion has its own ritual objects. Ours were: the thermometer, Omnadine, an all-purpose vaccine lost to the years, tea enemas, muddy oozing Argyrol nose drops, a demitasse cup of squeezed beef juice, against anemia (where was cholesterol?), Cascara pills and the croup kettle whose wet chuckle is as archaic today as the raw blast of the ram's horn sounded inside the synagogue. Dr. Stieglitz's edicts were commandments: bed rest until the mercury in the thermometer registered below 100° (rectal) for at least thirty-six hours; on a fine day, during convalescence, a brief stroll on the sunny side of the street at high noon; daily bowel movements; at night, the window opened only a crack, woolen underwear during the winter; at all seasons, avoidance of crowds because of contagion. The doctor's personal demons consisted of: kidney disease (at some point, all his patients had been threatened by that dread diagnosis), sinus infections, drafts, the appendix—I imagined this treacherous organ as a hot coal ready to erupt into conflagration at any moment—and the ineptness of other physicians, with the exception of an occasional specialist of Dr. Stieglitz's own choosing, picked for his manual dexterity. They were the carpenters, engineers, plumbers and plasterers of the medical profession. His joy lay in the passionate loyalty of his followers, his favorites being ladies, preferably pretty and wealthy. And just as a fond father dandles his infant upon his knee, the doctor took pleasure in catering to the nervous breakdowns and amorous misadventures of his helpless female patients. ". . . And there I found her," he related, "with a smoking pistol still in her hand. Fortunately, her lover had suffered only superficial flesh wounds . . ."

In my mind's eye, I created a tragic silent movie: the leading lady, wild eyed, her long hair undone, cascading over the shoulders of her lace negligee, and, sprawled on a bear rug at her feet, the erring male—dead.

Dr. Stieglitz's office was his temple. The patients sat in the drab, windowless waiting room, hopeful as pilgrims at Lourdes, for they knew there was no other place of cure. I, for one, had never set foot inside a hospital until I was more than twenty years of age, and the postponed experience had been as traumatic as would be a visit to Dante's hell. Now, when I walk along upper Park Avenue, I still resent the interloper's name outside Dr. Stieglitz's office. For me, the building is in ruins but, in my fancy, I restore the well-known ground floor space to its original state. I see again the frugal, homely furnishings and the high priest who officiated over them in his white smock, with his sterile white goatee and black eyes endowed with their penetrating x-ray vision. The door of his waiting room was divided horizontally, the upper section remaining open for ventilation without drafts. It reminded me of the entrance to a stable and I could picture an equine head peering through it. The patients sat, uncomfortably, on hardwood seats, listening to a concert of coughs, sneezes and snufflings. Then, what about contagion? In that sanctified ambiance, its demonic powers were neutralized. From the inner sanctum could be heard the ominous, mechanical stutter of the suction machine pumping some unfortunate's sinuses. I sometimes wonder to what clinical other-world that instrument of torture has been relegated.

In the doctor's private office, I remember, chiefly, the reproduction in blacks and grays of Rembrandt's painting, *The Anatomy Lesson*, hanging on a wall above his desk. It showed a group of scientific savants gathered around a corpse. These pictorial physicians, long dead, covered by the dignified patina of history, unlike the doctor's living colleagues, were received in his office with due respect.

The examining room was dominated by the leather surgical table at center; in retrospect it appears as abnormally large and ungainly as a dinosaur. All around, on shelves behind glass doors, like old-fashioned kitchen cabinets, a collection of occult instruments were arranged. The doctor's sole helper was Miss Marks, an unorthodox assistant, neither nurse, secretary nor receptionist—yet she was all of them and more—and qualified for the position through fanatical devotion to her employer. Homely as a crow, she always wore a black sweater sprinkled with ashes from an omnipresent cigarette, extinguished only when, acting as the doctor's right hand, she proffered the tools of his profession.

When I think back to the hours spent in this temple of medicine, I remember, uncomfortably, the exorcism rites for the routing of sinusitis. The doctor, appetizing in his freshly laundered laboratory coat, with his rosy, scrubbed complexion, polished bald pate and trademark white swab on his chin, looked too immaculate for the nasty combat with nasal bacterial demons. He would sit squarely facing the patient, straddling a standard swivel stool. In later years, a minor paunch could be detected, but it looked trim, like all else about his person. The treatment was messy and inexorable, always unpleasant; and despite familiarity and trust in its efficacy, I squirmed as much as the hard seat would allow. First, a series of sprays were squirted into nose and throat to dilate reluctant passages; this was followed by the insertion into the nostril cavities of two toothpicks wrapped in cotton, saturated with magic Argyrol. One sat helplessly, like a trapped rhinoceros with stick tusks, until the medicament was absorbed; at which point, no amount of tissue could sop up the frontal seepage, while the backward drip tasted of bitter gall.

Now, thus prepared, one was ready to endure the final, most violent phase of the ritual; the suction apparatus was put to work. The patient intoned the prescribed mantra, chanting "K . . . K . . . K . . ." to keep the eustachian passages open, thus preventing deafness from the assault. It felt as though one's brains were being blown out, collected along with the slimy mucous in the transparent glass receptacle. But the doctor exulted over the amount of "muck" he had extracted. And when my bib was removed and I was released at last, I felt supernaturally cleansed and clear as I floated down Park Avenue, buoyant as a sprite.

By far, the most interesting area of Dr. Stieglitz's office was a windowless nook, containing a shabby couch and his rickety metabolism machine, the latter another vanished species today. This model was partially homemade because when I lay on the couch dutifully breathing "naturally" at the doctor's command, I watched my inhaling and exhaling registered by the gentle rise and fall of a cylinder that had once served as a cookie tin. On the wall before me, I was privileged to view a print of Böcklin's *Isle of Death*, the island surrounded by spiky cemetery cypress, with a small boat steered by Charon making its way toward this sinister final destination. The representation of this allegory might seem inappropriate to a doctor's office, but in this particular sanctuary it was deprived of its morbidity. Furthermore, for me, the metabolism room had a different, more interesting use. I knew that it served as a clandestine meeting place for lovers. Here, upon this moldy couch, couples (acquaintances of the doctor's), lacking any other shelter, consummated their passions. Dr. Stieglitz, always a champion of romance, was as indulgent towards others as he was in regard to himself. So, as I lay on the couch attached to the primitive metabolism assemblage, faced by the picture of *Isle of Death*, my dreamy, adolescent fancy agreeably roamed elsewhere.

Leopold Stieglitz survived into his eighties. For a brief period following his eightieth birthday, he retired from practice, closing his office and deserting the "faithful," leaving us to the unsupervised blunders of the "plumbers," the "carpenters," the "engineers" and the "plasters." When we asked him to recommend a replacement, he could give us no help. But we knew beforehand that there was no other. "He's all right if you don't mind a bit of stupidity" or "with him, you must accept the fact that golf comes first . . . ," he might say when the reputation of some doctor was placed before him. There was a sardonic twinkle in his jet eyes, but they seemed also to be telling us, mutely, "You will just have to be brave." The deprived period was brief and, despite acute angina and palsy that caused his right hand to tremble uncontrollably, the doctor returned to our midst.

He continued to pay house calls. After my marriage, when he came to our brownstone during the winter season, he would sit in his chauffeur-driven limousine, while Miss Marks stepped out first to see that the door was open and that the doctor would have minimum exposure to the elements. Then, slowly, the doctor would emerge, carrying his black satchel, swathed in a variety of wool scarves, sweaters and overcoats (according to the weather) that he would remove hastily inside our warm foyer. His bedside manner remained unchanged and, despite his hostility to the cold, he brought with him the freshness of outdoors recalled from my childhood illnesses. Although his motions were slow, they appeared more deliberate than feeble; his skin was still ruddy and firm and his black eyes brilliant. But the presence of Josephine Marks hovered around him, a somber, protective acolyte.

As he no longer had an office, we made medical visits to his apartment, where he treated us in the living room, a cluttered place of overstuffed Victorian furniture and knickknacks. It was said that the Chinese urn on the mantel contained the ashes of Amanda, his lady love, (later, briefly, his wife). I did not question this unscientific, arcane observance any more than I did the modern art in the doctor's conventional, old-fashioned home. In the place of honor above the mantel, adjacent to the Chinese vase, was a painting by Georgia O'Keeffe: a magnified flower, executed in bold color, its fleshy petals open to reveal its inner parts, sexual and female. O'Keeffe's innovative creations had caused prudish shock when they were introduced by her husband, Alfred Stieglitz, the renowned photographer, gallery owner and self-made eccentric philosopher of aesthetics—Leopold's older brother. But the doctor's patients grew to be on intimate terms with the works of O'Keeffe, Marin, Dove and Hartley, members of Alfred's group. While most of us had been unaccustomed to the avant-garde, on the doctor's walls these pictures became a type of family portraiture. And just as the heavy pendulous lower lips, the elongated faces of Spanish royalty painted by Goya, illustrate the dynasty's special genetic traits, the examples of art from Alfred Stieglitz's collection found in his brother's home attested to the uniqueness of the Stieglitz clan, in which the solid bourgeois was leavened by an inherited susceptibility to aesthetics. Leopold's sister resembled the actress Eleanora Duse; she had the doctor's black eyes, overhung by a luxuriant swag of hair. I was told that she once aspired to the stage but, failing that, she now boasted of her friendships with the great of theatre and opera. It was even rumored that Enrico Caruso had kissed the hem of her long, brocaded skirt. Leopold played the violin, an ardent amateur, and I was certain that Julius, who shared with his twin every twinge of pain, must have been musically gifted also.

During those last years, I would extend myself, obediently, on the doctor's green velvet sofa, while he lowered himself laboriously to his knees beside me, a syringe in his wavering right hand. But my relief at his return was so great that I took little notice of his humble posture. Nor did I feel any concern about the circuitous route or the landing place of the needle—would it be eye, ear, or, happily, my exposed waiting buttock?

There must have been a final meeting, but as it was unanticipated, it went unnoticed at the time. I never really believed that the doctor could die. And so, bulletins on his last illness reached me with no more immediacy than a newspaper story about a volcanic eruption on some unimaginable, distant island. His angina had worsened, causing great pain, and he remained at home, nursed only by Josephine Marks, his faithful slave. Still distrusting the medical blunderers, in the main, he treated his malady himself. But at last, in his ninetieth year, he let go. Even then, I pushed away the thought of his death. Perhaps to compensate for this cowardice, I keep a stubborn memory of an official salute to his demise. I am not, however, certain that it is real. Might it merely be a dream that upon awakening I have never been able to dispel?

I find myself in a funeral parlor seated beside my father who is eighty-seven, and who will die, also, within the year. I see the coffin smothered in roses, and I wonder at this misuse of blooming nature, just as I resent the ersatz homeyness of these secular mortuary mansions, sops to unbelievers to soften the blow of death. But would Dr. Stieglitz, who had made it an inflexible rule throughout his life never to attend a patient's funeral, have allowed one for himself? Would he have submitted to a public capitulation to his adversary? I glance at my father. What is he thinking? His old friend is dead and he will be next. But his expression is composed, he is still very much of this earth, and I reach for the comfort of his hand. But when both were gone, I felt abandoned, a small bark, unmoored, sailing upon indifferent waters.

Chapter Six

SUBSTITUTE MOTHERS

The things we learn through family lore may assume a patina of lived experience resembling personal memories. For this reason, the wet nurse who suckled me appears as someone I once knew: her large breasts sufficiently overflowing to nourish me, as well as her own offspring, my "milk sibling" (a connection never mentioned). It is astonishing that this archaic maternal figure managed to endure well into the twentieth century when fashionable obstetricians recommended her services to their cossetted patients from New York City's upper bourgeoisie. In my mind's eye, I see these new mothers recuperating in their own soft beds with embroidered pillows and sheets (hospitals were used, rarely, for deliveries), while a stranger stood by to assuage their infant's cries of hunger. Were women biologically different, then, or were they merely more assiduous in the preservation of their youthful contours, lacking the contemporary restoratives of gymnasiums, jogging and aerobic dancing? Surely the latter did not apply to my mother who was without feminine vanity. Perhaps physi-

cians with their professional right to change their minds
were convinced, in those days, that the milk of their
wealthy, urban clientele was thin, scant and blue compared
to the copious, creamy output of some hired country
woman. Whatever the case, custom, an erratic tyrant, had
introduced the wet nurse at the scene of my birth.

The trained babies' nurse is found on the opening
page of a photograph album: a starched mannequin with a
small package—me—on her knees. Beneath the snapshot,
in painstaking script, my mother had inscribed my name,
weight, date and hour of birth, as though, largely unemployed in my behalf, she had taken up her pen as the loving
biographer of her own infant. I know merely impersonal
data concerning this white-capped professional: her name
and the fact that she was British, an asset for her breed. In
the picture, her face is obscure and her stay was too brief to
impress her personality in the family log.

She was followed by two German sisters, and, just as
for an anthropologist the discovery of the traces of some
primitive tribe is a clue to primeval times, Clara and Frida
Lund represent the dawn of first recall. I place them in a
nursery furnished in white wicker just as early man is
presented in his cave at the Museum of Natural History. It
is summer and the window shades are lowered against the
sun's assault at the rest hour. But, at night, my brother and
I sleep outdoors on a screened porch late into the season; in
defiance of frost. I see us—two grotesque shapes bundled
into layers of heavy clothing, silhouettes resembling astro-
nauts, undreamed of at that date. The Lund sisters believed
fervently in fresh air. They themselves looked as though
they had just come indoors from a field in their native

Bavaria, where they had been pitching hay. Plump and rosy, they had flaxen hair coiled and pinned into a rustic architecture of braids and top-knots. Their departure was sudden, under a cloud of mystery, and despite the cheerfulness of their double portrait in the background there is an undefined shadow, murky, sinister, unfading.

The Lund sisters were replaced by Fraulein Iska, a governess, a step forward in the evolution of substitute mothers. She was erudite, able to recite, by heart, the works of Goethe, Schiller and Heine, but even a five-year-old, without knowledge of the medical term, was able to diagnose her as an hysteric. With the quirky persistence of memory I always picture her, seated between my brother and me, on the back seat of our commodious Pierce Arrow automobile. I see her in gaunt profile, with a long nose and a receding chin, her bony hands clasped in terror as she screams, "*Nicht so schnell!*" at our uncomprehending, placid Irish chauffeur. Miss Iska was subject to back pains and I retain another image from that period, framed inside a keyhole, as I peep into the sickroom where a strange young doctor who looked like Ronald Coleman is treating her. At this moment, he is found on the floor, his long legs pointing ceilingward, a hypodermic needle still clutched in his hand, my child's desk chair having collapsed beneath his weight, splintering its dismembered parts over the carpet. Miss Iska, from the bed, looks on in horror, a major player in this slapstick film, and her shrieks are a discordant accompaniment because no matter how ill she never lost her power of vigorous vocal complaint.

Several governesses came and went and were forgotten before the arrival of Mademoiselle Hélène Raymonde, who presided over my childhood and early adolescence. A foreign bird, she roosted among us for many years without becoming assimilated into the family coop; I no longer recall the day of her entrance into our lives. By what route will that stately person emerge from the past?

Not long ago, a friend, knowing that I had sold my set of the Bibliothèque Rose and regretted it, gave me one volume from the series of old-fashioned novels for children by the Russian-born Countess de Ségur. These books being all but unavailable now, he had come across this single copy of *Les petites filles modeles*, in a secondhand book store on the Left Bank. I held it, a treasure, and imbibed its special pink color—a blend of beet juice and rose petals. Like a blind person, I ran my hands over the cover with the embossed name of the publisher, Hachette, and the title, set in an armorial design. The aristocratic famous lady author's name is found, inconspicuously, inside on the first page. With this volume in hand, just as a mountain peak pierces the fog, out of forgetfulness the top of Mademoiselle's head came into view: her curled bang, heavy black brows and dark blue eyes—deprived of their intrinsic beauty because they were located on that particular face. I opened the book and was met by the odor, musty, pleasant and nostalgic of old libraries—the same one I would experience on my return from Central Park on late winter afternoons, when Mademoiselle sat down to read out loud from the Bibliothèque Rose. Those eighteenth century tales were more fascinating than any contemporary American fiction for children, because of their improbable realism and the exoticism of those little French aristocrats and their adventures. The black-and-white illustrations show their faces, old as their guardians, whose quaint moralities required them to be either sadistically punitive or tearfully sentimental in their dealings with their charges, a population of old-young prankish dwarfs! In *Les petites filles modeles*, there is a picture of a privileged child cradling a doll, a perfect miniature of herself, dressed in long skirt and buttoned boots, while a peasant girl with two loaves of bread under her arms looks on with envy. The caption reads: *"Elle est tout de même jolie votre poupée."* The inequality of class was never sidestepped by the Countesse de Ségur. Now Mademoiselle Raymonde stands before me in clear detail from head to foot. She is tall and well proportioned, as far as one can tell, because she is camouflaged, winter and summer, by an excess of clothing. In her exaggerated *pudeur* (inadequately translated, modesty), the body was a shameful necessity, to be hidden at all times from intrusive eyes. Only her face and a bit of upper chest were ever exposed, the latter more revealing than any bikini-clad bather, as it was the barometer of her suppressed emotions. She always wore a tiny diamond pendant and, just like the evening star at ruddy sunset, it twinkled, cool and white, against the fierce blush of Mademoiselle's chest that expressed anger, embarrassment or any other strong, unwanted feeling.

Mademoiselle carried with her three environments, including the present one, with us; and just as a juggler keeps his colored balls aloft, simultaneously, she managed to conserve her various attachments at the same time. There was her aunt, old now, retired, but worshipped by her niece because she had known the overwhelming distinction of being governess to the family of the last Czar of Russia. Mademoiselle often brought out her pictures of that doomed group: the Ruler, with his imperial beard, the haughty, Germanic Czarina and the young princesses, all in white, their long hair caught back by large white bows that looked inappropriately frivolous and pathetic, like decorations when the party is over. And the little Czaravitch; in Mademoiselle's lamentings, his incurable hemophilia became history on a scale with the massacres of the Revolution. I loved and lost a small enamel egg, fashioned by Fabergé, the court jeweler, and given to Mademoiselle by her aunt.

For the *"petits McGustys,"* however, I felt only hostility, because not a day went by without Mademoiselle's extolling the superior qualities and endearing traits of the family she worked for before coming to us. "Bubby," her favorite, seemed more angel than school boy and Margery, her special responsibility, was pretty as a doll, with long blond curls, dimpled cheeks and a perpetually cheerful nature. The two oldest boys, away at college, were more vague, but no less perfect absentee demi-gods, while M. and Mme. McGusty represented the crowned heads of Washington Square. I grew to dislike, increasingly, "la famille McGusty," until, by some unknown maneuver on the part of Mademoiselle, I received an invitation to a birthday party in honor of Margery. My childish subconscious, distorted by the rarely mentioned fact that we were Jews, caused me to regard new people, Christians especially (the McGustys were Irish Catholics), as a challenge that combined with an amorphous fear of social failure. Although I cannot say that as an outsider I enjoyed this festivity, with only Mademoiselle as ambassadoress to represent me, her diamond pendant, like a decoration sparkling on her chest, turkey red from the emotion of this meeting between two nations, but the confrontation of *les petits McGustys*, in the flesh, did a great deal to dispel their myth. "Bubby" was chubby and lethargic and the birthday girl, examined with minute attention, was wearing an unbecoming dress of off-white net over canary taffeta that clashed with her yellow cork-screw curls and the tan freckles scattered over her pug's face. At home, my parents questioned me about the gathering and I remembered my father remarking, "Tammany Hall trash!" I had no notion what kind of insult this might be, but it, too, helped to dim the aura that had surrounded the McGustys although Mademoiselle's praises continued as enthusiastic as ever. I knew that Mademoiselle took pride in us, too, and I was certain that in her next position she would expound our superiority. But she disapproved of giving compliments, directly, and the one instance when she broke her rule was as outlandish as would be the sight of a nun in habit dancing to rock music! The purely physical was unmentionable, unthinkable and invisible: I do not believe that Mademoiselle had ever beheld even her own nude body. Her method of disrobing for bed consisted of an elaborate process of placing her opaque cotton nightgown, wide as a tent, over her daytime clothes and wriggling out of the latter, managing, somehow, never to reveal the smallest section of her uncovered person. So it came as a double surprise one evening when I was in the bath that she cast a connoisseur's eye over me, and said, "You will be all right, you are going to be a *fause maigre*" (false thin). The phrase remains untranslatable, but flattering to this very moment.

The geography of Central Park is unchanged since

my childhood, but its population has altered. It is now a recreational haven during twelve months of the year, for all ages, classes and ethnic groups. Then, it served chiefly, as the appointed meeting ground for a cluster of clubs of European governesses. The Ramble, a wooded section, was used by Irish nursemaids; a short passage located at the southern end of the Park, called Donkey Hill, was appropriated by frauleins; while at the Mall, French was spoken. Perhaps, this broad asphalt boulevard lined with bronze busts of the dead great on marble pedestals reminded the homesick women of the swath of the Champs-Élysées and the cultivation of their own heroes and intellectual giants. I rediscovered my "park friends" every afternoon after school; and just as in the garden of some European hotel, the intimacies of American children are both swift and rootless, these contacts unlike those derived from home and classrooms, were close but temporary, depending on the gathering in Central Park of our foreign substitute mothers. In the fall, we played hopscotch amid fallen leaves, crinkled and crisp as breakfast cornflakes; in winter, our cheeks were whipped rosy by the cutting edge of an icy wind, and, in the lassitude of spring, we said tearful farewells for the summer.

Just as violins can be heard tuning discreetly in an orchestra pit, on the benches, the governesses gossiped in undertones. But every now and then, a solo command would ring out loudly:

"Jeanne, do not skate out of sight!"

"Rachele, include your little brother, please."

The voices of the French mademoiselles are silent now, but their ghosts still hover around the impassive, enduring bronze statues of the famous.

As with her entrance, I no longer recall Mademoiselle Raymonde's exit from my life. But odd moments
adhere to memory: Mademoiselle singing snatches of favorite arias from Bizet's opera, *Carmen*. With the unanalytical
literalness of childhood, I never wondered why this prudish
spinster was attracted to the musical declamations of the
passionate, fickle gypsy. In retrospect, the curly bang, the
dignified overgarbed silhouette of Mademoiselle are associ-
ated, oddly, with the façade of the Paris Opera House,
monumental, historic, smothered in decoration—I have a
vision clear and surreal as a dream of Mademoiselle, her
décolletage colored carmine from unaccustomed exercise,
tossing a balloon back and forth with me in an indoor
version of badminton. I see her watching over the wavering
lines of my cross-stitching on a pillow intended for my
mother's birthday; the detested occupation made bearable
because I made believe that I was acting a part out of the
Bibliothèque Rose.

Shortly after her departure, we learned the astound-
ing news of Mademoiselle's marriage to a retired school
teacher! An unimaginable event that interested me not at all.
It is a mystery how someone who had lived so closely by my
side could drop away without any notice. Did I, then, feel
no affection for my old companion? Or, rather, after she
had gone, did she appear less a person than a phase; a period
that I had outgrown, like, on a wall, last season's pencil
mark that denoted this year's increased height?

This spring as I sat in the Tuileries Gardens, gazing
at the long vista stretching to the Arc de Triomphe, I saw
Mademoiselle Raymonde coming towards me. I recognized

the crimped fringe, the tall, dignified form swaddled in those old-fashioned, concealing garments. But I searched, in vain, for the young charge by her side; this woman walked alone. Only then, did I remember that Mademoiselle must have been long dead—and that she was "Madame," name unknown—at the time of her demise. And I felt slightly cheated that no child after me had heard the praises of my perfections as I had endured those of *"les petits McGustys"* in the days of my childhood.

When I was a child, Bini's room was a haven; home from school I ran there. I would stand at the threshold, absorbing the clutter and confusion I knew so well. Bini's past and my mother's were perpetuated here and I was able to sort the strands or roll them together in a colorful blend. The room was small and faced a blank courtyard wall. Near the window was a bureau with snapshots of Bini's family in France: a picture of a first communion that looked bridal, a wretched bride (Bini's niece and namesake, Alice) that looked like a first communion, another of a small gable-roofed house at the edge of a wood—the house where Bini was born. A framed yellowing photograph of her parents had a sprig of dried wildflowers and a four-leaf clover under the glass. The bureau was covered by an embroidered hand towel and an ivory brush, comb, and mirror set was neatly laid out. Near these, a box that looked like a miniature coffin enclosed Bini's rosary, handsome in jet with a mother-of-pearl cross.

Bini sat by the window in a rocker, sewing, with her feet on a discarded crate. She always saved everything: "Who knows what might not come in useful?" She held her wicker sewing basket in her lap. It contained many treasures. There was a pin cushion shaped like a tomato, studded with pins of varying size and shape, a darning egg of smooth celluloid, and a tape measure that snapped into its case like a recoiling asp. When you put your face inside Bini's sewing basket, the cretonne lining smelled of lavender, spice and age. I used to watch the darning egg slide down the long throat of my mother's stocking. "Bini, tell me a story," I said.

"*Allez, allez,* can't you see I'm busy now?" she would answer with good-natured brusqueness. "If you keep on interrupting me how will I ever earn my pension and retire to Champagney and my rose garden?"

I had heard this too often to be deterred by it. "Tell me about your family-in-France," I said as I had so many times before.

Bini's family-in-France belonged with the figures in a Gallic fairy tale. Her father had been a forester; to me that meant someone who chopped wood in a jerkin and boots in a thick forest evil with spotted toadstools. One of her brothers had been a priest; I always pictured him on a bicycle riding through the narrow streets of her hometown, wearing a padre hat and, uncomfortably, a cassock that hid his legs and feet. He had a long loaf of bread for the poor tucked under his arm.

"You have heard about my family so often. They are just plain people," Bini said.

"Tell me just once more how you came to Grandmother's house off the boat from France."

"That was a long time ago. I was pretty then, your Maman always said so. I wore a white shirtwaist held high

at the throat by dressmaker's bones and a hat with blue
flowers that matched my eyes . . . *eh bien, tout change, tout
casse, tout, sauf le souvenir. . . .*"

I reveled in Bini's sentimental reminiscences. I
never tired of hearing about her "chances." She had been
engaged to an Irish coachman named Patrick—"as strong as
a lion, yet he died of flu in the epidemic." Then, when she
was traveling with my grandparents, the proprietor of the
best hotel in Berlin had proposed to her. "He was very
rich" she always said with a slight note of regret in her
voice. He had followed her all over Europe, but she had
remained firm. "What, marry a Boche!" she had said. "And
live in that *sale pays!* Never! Better to be the old maid I am."

But she never seemed like an old maid to me. She
was too individual to be classified and I knew her too well.

After Bini left my family to live with her married
niece in her hometown, Champagney, her letters arrived
regularly on ceremonial occasions: birthdays, Christmas,
New Year, anniversaries. Her small, firm, pointed writing
that looked like fine lace was a link with the past. Sometimes, after my mother's death, she would confuse generations, so that I became Alma and my mother Madame
Wallach. She was always nostalgic for my family and I
suspected that now that she had at last retired and left the
United States forever, we seemed more her own than her
niece and her husband with whom she made her home. Her
letters made clearings in forgetfulness: I saw Bini wrapping
her blue kimono printed with tiny Japanese lanterns around
her heavy legs marbled with old veins, as she prepared to
climb into an upper berth, "I wish you would let me sleep
up there. "*Va t'en!* This is the way I always traveled. I'm not

giving up yet"; Bini cleaning the gravy on her plate with a crust of bread with the same vigor I had seen her use in attacking dust in corners with a broom; offering me Jordan almonds, tasting like sugar-coated wood, that she always kept in her room for afternoon "*goûtés*"; Bini's lurid *True Story* magazines and her recitals of the plot of the movie she had seen on Thursday, her "day off."

During World War II I received a letter for my birthday. I saved it because of its characteristic blend of courage, materialism, good sense, and sentiment. It was written like all her letters, in an original combination of French and French-English.

> Here we are at your *anniveraire* once again. How the time passes, especially when you are getting old. Seventy years is approaching but I have my health and that is the essential.
>
> I am remembering all the anniversaries I passed with you and I am asking myself what you are doing. Yes, the years go on and my thoughts often go back to when your Papa and Maman were engaged. I was very much touched that they were telling me right away. I have been part of your family since before that time. I have a nice remembrance of everyone. I had a beautiful collection of postal cards of all the countries we went to but the Germans took them all. Nevertheless I have the remembrance. I remember many things—your Maman used to speak to me of my pension for my old age. "I don't want you to have to worry when you are old, Alice," she used to say. My dear niece, Alice, and her good Gaston would take care of me. Just the same it's nice to have your own.
>
> We are all well, *Grâce à Dieu*. Gaston is home now. He has not started to repair the inside of the house due to the fact that you cannot get material, but when it will be possible he will start it. He is in no hurry as the outside is done now, at least we are covered. We eat well enough. We do not suffer

like the people of the city. All the same we ask each other when this terrible war will be finished.

Not long ago I had a little accident, *pas grande chose.* I was returning home with the ration when I was struck. *Grâce à Dieu,* I was carrying my wallet, WELL-FILLED, inside my *chemise* and the bullet was stopped, taking only a little piece of stomach. I was in the hospital in Belfort for two weeks. Now I am home again since a month and my health is good.

Remember me kindly to your Papa, *votre frère,* your cousins, Marian and Manfred. What good times we all had together. I will always think of the family Wallach with a full heart and gratitude. Salutations to *M. votre mari.* May you all keep safe. If you have a picture of your baby, please send it to me. How he must be big now! I remember when you were born and I lined a wash basket with pink silk because you arrived ahead of time and we were not ready. You were so small! How the years pass!

"Accept, *ma bien chère,* my very best felicitations on this occasion, also on the part of Alice and Gaston. May the next year bring you what your heart desires. *Je reste toujours votre bien affectionée,*

Bini

Alice Galland,

Champagney, Haute-Saône-France

The letters kept coming but they grew less cheerful. She had loved her niece as her last blood tie, but it became apparent that her love was not shared and it degenerated into a tyranny founded on the money she had contributed to the household through the years. More and more often she suggested we meet in Paris on one of my trips to Europe. "It would be like the old days with M and Mme Wallach." But the reunion never took place. Did I back away from the mortuary responsibility of representing those shadow figures out of the past? At the last minute, did Bini not wish to confirm her regrets? Or was it simply not practical? I do not know. But soon she grew too old to undertake the journey. Then another letter arrived.

> I am no longer living with Alice and Gaston. They have turned me out, after all my good care of them and money spent on their house! I am living in a *pension*. The landlady interests herself in me and the food is passable. I can't walk any more, my veins give me trouble. On good days I sit in the little garden in the rear that looks over the orchard which is bearing a good crop this year. And I dream of my years with your family . . .

I saw her, the same figure I remembered, in a rocking chair with her feet on a discarded packing case, but her legs are now wrapped in bandages like the burlap coverings around wintering shrubs. Her pompadour of dark hair is white, she has grown from comfortably plump to very heavy and there is no sewing basket in her lap. Her familiar rough hands are idle. Far away in place and time, the Wallach family is still parading through her mind. They keep her company.

After my son's marriage I wrote Bini and enclosed a newspaper clipping of the event for her memorabilia. But I never saw her writing again. "My aunt passed away on June first. I am told, peacefully. My husband joins me in thanking you for your generosity through the years. . . ."

The story of Bini's last years (she lived to be ninety-one and her retirement lasted twenty-three years) sounds like a Balzac novel, composed of all the tough, touching, sordid tragic elements of middle-class French life. She has grown unreal with the passage of time but I will not give her the face of fiction. I recall that small, dark back room filled with treasured objects: dried flowers, pin cushion, old photographs—from there she exhorts me to safeguard my past ". . . *tout change, tout casse, tout, sauf le souvenir* . . ."

"I won't forget," I reassure her. And I have kept my promise.

Chapter Seven

PROGRESSIVE HEADMISTRESS

As an archivist collects data from a past era, I might describe the educational ideals of Miss Helen Parkhurst, founder and principal of the *Dalton School,* in words such as: "experience," "activity," "growth," "process." But abstractions are inadequate for the reconstruction of those days, and I prefer the random pictures of memory. In recall, the headmistress looms large, a ponderous shape, neither feminine nor masculine, her face is ruddy and her features insignificant, engulfed by folds of flesh. Although she was neither lover of children nor books, just as sun and rain are necessary to the products of the soil, she was vital to the implantation and flourishing of her innovative liberating system of education. She came from the Middle West, an area more foreign to her New York City student body than India, the home of the over-life-sized Buddha statue that stood sentinel, in the "new building," outside her office door.

      The "old" school (called The Children's University) was situated on the West Side, around the corner from

Central Park. It consisted of two shabby brownstones joined at the rear by a covered wooden bridge. The rooms were furnished sketchily with the discards of an obsolete domesticity. The headmistress frowned upon all standard scholastic equipment that might lead to the passive, coercive intake of knowledge. On my first morning at The Children's University after having suffered at a formal, restrictive school where the pupils were pinioned behind identical desks clamped to the floors, the cozy welcoming atmosphere was as reassuring to me as the lights over a cottage door to a wayfarer lost in the night. Boys and girls of all ages (arbitrary division by class had been abolished) lay stretched out on cushions beneath bay windows; reading, composing stories or merely daydreaming. On a wicker fan-tail chair, a girl with curly hair was writing busily. I peered at the pad on her knees and read:

. . . then by the light of the moon, they danced, slowly around the Sphinx.

The words are indelible, and so many years later, they still seem to be poetic magic.

In the history "laboratory" (the oddly clinical word was used in place of "classroom" to connote the experimental nature of the school). Was it an intended tribute to the new supremacy of Science or, to Miss Parkhurst, were we all guinea pigs in her own grand plan? A "conference" was underway, and a group of young "China experts" was clustered around a scarred table that in a former incarnation might have been used for nursery meals. What the students lacked in factual information was made up for by their clamorous enthusiasm. I remember the stiff raising of an arm in response to a question from the pedagogue on a dais in my old classroom, while, here, the teacher was seated in the midst of her students. In retrospect, I see her as a female King Lear, her gray hair in wild disarray, surrounded by daughters (and sons) unimpressed by the superiority of her years.

The literature laboratory was an alcove off a larger room that served as library and the site of the milk and graham crackers ceremony at eleven o'clock. The English teacher's realm was a dusky cave lit by her presence. Tall and thin as a candle, she had the head of an emperor on an ancient coin, with aristocratic features and close-cropped curls, ill matched to her long, droopy tie-dye skirts and the brown wool socks and sneakers she wore at all seasons. When she read aloud from the *Iliad, Odyssey, Arabian Nights, Beowolf* and *King Arthur and His Knights*, the heroes from those pages were more real to us than the shadowy shapes of automobiles and pedestrians on the street outside.

The sensation of wood planks beneath my feet brings back the bridge connecting the two brownstones of the Children's University School. Over the roofed passageway, we trooped to the assembly room, a converted basement, where pipes crawled across the ceiling, rickety folding chairs slithered over the dusty cement floor and naked bulbs did little to alleviate a perpetual demi-light. Yet the stage, a shallow elevation separated from the audience by a drawstring curtain, was the very heart of the school— the proving ground and culminating point of experiential education. Here, we acted out our own plays based upon our own discoveries in history and literature; and it was here in the auditorium that I felt the first symptoms of romantic love. The object was a boy older than I, president of the student government, blond, broad shouldered, athletic. Even his name, Nicol Bissel, unforgettable, resonated with a special sound. When he stood at the center of the front row, the rest of the chorus grouped around him, it was his voice I singled out, and it seemed to be directed straight towards me as he sang,

> I got shoes, you got shoes, all God's chillun got shoes, when I get to Heben I gonna put on my shoes, I gonna walk all over God's Heben . . .

Today, with our self-conscious ethnic credos, it seems impossible that any school would permit a young Nordic Adonis and an all-white choir to perform this program—to mimic Negro spirituals, their rhythms and speech—pilfering a culture that belonged to another race.

When the singing stopped, I was crying, overwhelmed, I believed, by empathy for the plight of the slaves we had discussed in history conference. Only later, did I realize that it had been Nicol Bissel, and not the chant, that had produced the tears from the untapped well of my emotions.

Those two old brownstones (long demolished) have passed into legend, and the "new" building, still standing, is history to me now, improbable and anachronistic. This structure looks no different from its neighbors, the apartment buildings along upper Park Avenue. Miss Parkhurst, as usual, pitted against the current, chose the early 1930s, the Depression years, to make the costly move. A wealthy family, her backers from the start, was called upon again and, in gratitude for their renewed generosity, the school was renamed Dalton, after the site of their thriving paper mill in Massachusetts. In my mind's eye, I see the headmistress, hefty as a truck farmer, proudly showing prospective fathers, successful New York City professionals and entrepreneurs (mainly, Jewish), around the unfinished building. They responded by enclosing her vision in solid brick.

For a while I felt the displacement as a loss. I disliked, actively, the subterranean swimming pool and the yellow-tiled gymnasium under the roof. The large, elaborate auditorium boasted a real stage with professional lighting and a sumptuous scarlet curtain that matched the rows of theatre seats. The carpeting was thick and the ceiling black and shiny as patent leather. In the new school, the headmistress had a proper office and her presence was less amorphous than in the early days, when at any moment, she might materialize like a pagan god descending to earth in human form. Now she was visited by appointment. My mother accompanied me for the ritual reading of the report card, and the embarrassing intrusion of a parent into school life was furthered by the inarticulateness of the headmistress. I felt secure in her approval, but her small, wise eyes, embedded in flesh, avoided mine, and the amenities of the meeting were left to my mother. We received written "remarks" instead of grades, and although it was pleasing to learn that I had a "beautiful soul" and a "fiercely independent mind," just as a vegetarian may long, occasionally, for red meat, there were moments when I would have preferred to know my marks, suppressed by Miss Parkhurst because they led to the dangers of competition—inimical to the joys of learning for learning's sake.

Although, at first, the new building seemed strange, the faculty, as before, was unorthodox, stimulating and heterogeneous. Like a band of pioneers, they followed their leader and they fill the mirror of memory with color. I recall Dr. Boris Bogoslovsky, a former Russian student revolutionary, who turned the science laboratory, with its dismembered frogs and mortuary smell of formaldehyde, into a clandestine political rendezvous. I watched him closely, as he shuffled from microscope to Bunsen burner to dissecting table, a stooped vaguely apologetic, lonely figure, who wore his rimless spectacles at the end of his long nose.

Shakespeare and Milton were taught by a Brahmin with ebony skin and chiseled features. His lips were full, sensuous and as finely modeled as a corolla, his eyes secret pools of blackness. Although he addressed his subject matter from a distance, a hint of the occult now and then, was enough to make me shiver with the desire to penetrate the mysteries of his Hindu transcendentalism. Is it only in imagination that I see him confronting his occidental pupils, his slight body effortlessly curled in the lotus position?

Now, new customs made their appearance for no apparent reasons: We marched to assembly in formation—shortest first, tallest last; and any visitor seeing the orderly file might have thought he was in an ordinary institution. Although there were still no desks in the laboratories, a blackboard did occasionally insinuate itself upon a gaily painted wall, and the generous rooms, identical in shape, also, suggested the conventional. A more radical change was the introduction of the IQ (Intelligence Quotient) tests. Lacking experience in taking examinations (they, too, fostered competition), I was terrified at being confronted with forms passed around by Dr. Genevieve Coy, the school psychologist, a stout woman, with straw-colored hair and a brisk expressionless voice, who reminded me of a warden; she actually blew a police whistle to signal the moment to start and again when our time was up. I became so rattled that I could hardly follow the printed directions and the answers, T, for true, F, for false, were a nightmare alphabet impossible to master after the heady freedom of self-expression. Like a patient in an examining room whose hospital smock slips, now here, now there, to reveal her shivering nudity, I feared that Dr. Coy's IQ tests would show up gaps in my knowledge, largely overlooked by the faith of the headmistress who believed that all children, given the proper environment for growth, possessed a touch of genius.

Despite these inroads, Miss Parkhurst's theories remained intact; but just as a farmer grown rich and successful may use his extended acreage to cultivate a garden of fantastic clipped hedges and experiment in the breeding of hybrid plants, her implementation became increasingly exotic. On her return from China, where she had introduced "progressive" education, the headmistress decided to create a "Meditation Room" on East Eighty-ninth street in New York. The retreat was blue (the color of thought), blue walls, ceiling and carpeting, and it was bare of furniture. At any hour of the day, we were encouraged to enter the sanctuary for renewal and inspiration. But high school girls, unindocrinated in the ways of the East, gathered squatting on the floor of the Meditation Room to giggle and tell "dirty" jokes. An admitted failure, it was closed down and converted to a nurse's station, for bodily needs instead of spiritual.

The headmistress, a quasi-acknowledged lesbian,

had never known the joys and trials of a family of her own. It would have been no more incongruous to see the Buddha statue cradling an infant in its arms than to think of Miss Parkhurst (whose concern was for children in general), as a mother. Nevertheless, she decreed that adolescent girls should experience, in advance, the pragmatic skills of the nursery. I had given little thought to babies since I stopped playing with dolls, and sex, overwhelmingly interesting, seemed disconnected from procreation—a merely biological term, a by-product, reserved for a later time. Yet, every few weeks, in rotation, feeling self-important in our starched white uniforms, the high school girls reported for duty at the sunny top floor creche, fortunately supervised by a professional. The blended smells of scalded milk, the rubber of sterilized nipples, talcum powder and urine accompany my recall of that venture. But, like most things shrouded in the future, motherhood was not to be imagined, and when it did arrive it found me green and uncertain as though I had never prepared a formula nor changed a diaper in the Dalton School nursery.

A slide stuck in a projector may appear again and again, and when I summon my memories of school, a certain picture shows up with like insistence. It presents a child standing at the corner of a stage, dwarfed by the backdrop of the tall folds of a scarlet curtain. Sound effects have been added to the scene and I hear an immature voice intoning in a single breath:

> The Lord is in his Holy Temple—let all the world keep silence before him.

The Oriental invocation is automatic, and it is blotted out by the mundane announcements that follow it. To this assemblage, the solemn prayer is quotidian, no more awesome than the fact that last night has passed, ceding its place to the minted freshness of another school day.

Now, when I pass the ten-story red brick building, I feel no connection. The ideologies of Miss Parkhurst, like seeds sown on the wind, have settled upon other schools, and without her inspiration and fanaticism, it is probable that Dalton, today, is no longer the place I knew. I did return, once, and discovered that, on the second floor, some branches of apple blossoms had been substituted for the presiding Buddha. Did assembly still open with that Oriental invocation, I wondered. In the lobby, I spotted students carrying academic school bags and wearing sweat shirts emblazoned with aggressive school lettering. Had competition, that unwelcome intruder, been admitted, at last, to Dalton?

Years after my graduation, a solemn march down the aisle (under the school banner with its motto Go Forth Unafraid) to the triumphant chords of the Russian national anthem, I heard that Miss Parkhurst had been dismissed by her board of directors, for mishandling funds. Despite the remoteness of our relationship, I felt a personal sadness at the thought of her departure. Where was she living? What was she doing? How could she be exercising her nurturing power?

Sacred elephants do not retire—they become extinct.

Chapter Eight

OLD MAIDS

I. MISS NELLY

In my mother's room there was a mahogany dressing table, kidney shaped, with slender, straight legs, naked, without a frilly skirt to conceal them. The glass-topped surface of the table held only a brush, comb and a Lalique bottle containing a small amount of perfume, rarely used; the coquetry of a cosmetics display was absent. The dressing table had a three-part mirror so that one might contemplate one's reflection from every angle. Yet, I do not remember my mother spending much time before it; and as I try to recapture her face, I am confronted by total erasure in the clear triple planes. They remain blank as frames without pictures. As I move my recollection around the room, I encounter twin beds, eighteenth-century English reproductions, also innocent of feminine furbelows, and a massive piece of furniture, half wardrobe, half chest of drawers, standing guard between the windows whose buttercup yellow curtains and valances are imprinted at regular intervals with medallions of roses, like the plots in a formal English garden. And, just as someone might be pleased to have succeeded in growing blooms in a desert land, my mother took pride in these cheerful flowered drapes in the otherwise austere room. But I preferred the white frost ferns that winter etched on the window panes, and I spurned the homeliness of my mother's maroon flannel robe hanging on the bathroom door. Though I enumerate these surrounding objects, like an insomniac counting sheep in vain, I am incapable of returning my mother's presence to their midst.

Not long ago, however, I opened a bottle of castille soap shampoo, and the smell, clean to the degree of being medicinal (freshly laundered linen blended with the odor in old apothecary shops), like a genie, conjured up my mother sitting at her dressing table. Her long, graying blond hair, released, floats free below her shoulders, which are protected by a white bath towel. I am aware that she is beautiful, but her face in the mirror swims into view through a haze, like the misted window panes after the frost ferns have melted.

There is a discreet knock on the bedroom door, which opens timidly to admit Miss Nelly, the hairdresser, carrying her black bag, like a doctor's satchel. I am able to see her in clear focus: tall, thin, angular, flat-chested, wearing the same dark gray shirtwaist dress in all seasons. Her pale features are regular, chiseled; in her youth she had probably been handsome. But, just as a shell abandoned by the tide grows dull, neglected on the sand, for some reason, the hope of marriage had long ago receded for Miss Nelly and, in her forties, she was left behind to fade, to exist for the rest of her days as one of a species extinct today: the old maid.

As she begins to brush my mother's hair, it crackles

under her hands, the material of Miss Nelly's labor turning
into electricity. The ritual of the shampoo took place in the
bathroom wash basin, the font from which my mother
emerged wafting that faint incense of castille soap, persisting
through the years. I used to lie on a bed to watch the
performance, which never varied. First, the wet hair would
be dried vigorously with a towel, until it stood out soft, silky
and youthful. After which, Miss Nelly would heat her tongs
on her spirit lamp, a ceremony at once archaic and
scientific. The curling iron would then grasp its prey in hot
jaws, releasing it strand by strand, crimped as bent wire,
until the whole head was marcelled like a corrugated roof
top. After that, Miss Nelly folded the ends tenderly into a
heavy bun that weighed upon my mother's neck.

All the while, my mother and the hairdresser
chatted of trivial matters: the weather, the traffic, predic-
tions for a coming outbreak of winter grippe. But habit
(Miss Nelly arrived punctually at four each Friday afternoon) had created an intimacy between them in which I, a
third person, was largely ignored.

Therefore, it came as a surprise when my mother
asked one day, "Would you like Miss Nelly to curl your
hair, too?"

She knew that I was going to a costume party the
following afternoon and we had shopped together for the
Pierrot outfit I was to wear. Since then, I had admired it
many times, fingering its slippery black and white satin folds
hanging in my closet and imagining the effect I would make
with my neck encircled in the ruff, stiff as porcelain, my legs
lost in the wide pantaloons.

Although the pointed cap would conceal most of

my hair, I accepted my mother's offer with enthusiasm, as though the hair curling, like a puberty rite, would be a crossing of the line between the uncertainty of adolescence and what I believed to be the self-confidence of maturity, which achieved, would ensure my popularity at the masquerade.

Miss Nelly consulted the large, nickel Ingersoll watch on her fragile, brittle wrist and said that she guessed she had time to spare before her next appointment. It was a new idea to me that her services were rendered to anyone besides my mother.

Soon, I was bending over the baptismal basin, water trickling uncomfortably into my ears, a wash cloth held over my face, like a mask, to save my eyes from the mild emulsion of castille soap. When I raised my head, I noticed that, just as vines intertwine on a garden wall, the white enamel bowl was garlanded by stray hairs—gray-blond and brown, my mother's and mine—mingled in arcane ceremony. Now it was my turn to sit in front of the dressing table mirror while Miss Nelly heated the iron. Although it looked as threatening as a dentist's drill, I sat motionless, unflinching, the bath towel over my shoulders, waiting for the transformation to be wrought. The close scrutiny of the results, however, I was saving for when I would be alone in the privacy of my room.

Miss Nelly, proud of her skill, remarked over my head. "I think she is going to look very pretty, but it is a shame she doesn't favor you more."

I had heard this latter pronouncement before from others but it had always left me surprisingly undistressed. Perhaps this was due to the warmth of my mother's

approval and her apparent indifference to her own appearance. Also, for me, the gulf separating child from adult was
too wide to allow for the competitiveness reserved for my
peers.

My mother answered Miss Nelly, "I am not as
colorful as my daughter, and she already has great style."

But it was no use, Miss Nelly's words stung. Due to
the puberty rite of passage now underway, I was propelled
into a heretofore unknown daughter-mother rivalry.

The operation over, I rushed to my room, a haven
I had chosen to furnish with the feminine knickknacks so
conspicuously missing from my mother's. Its center,
though, was a set of books on my bedside table: the novels
of Alexandre Dumas. I had only to open one of these to be
transported to the historic French court—a romantic world
of kings, queens, courtiers, courtesans and scheming red-
robed cardinals. Neither the rattle and tremor of the trains
beneath Park Avenue, nor the domestic hum of the vacuum
cleaner in the next room, not even the sound of key in latch
announcing my father's arrival home from the office could
disturb me, or make the halls of the Louvre palace disappear.

With a high heart, I went to the mirror to view my
new self. More disfiguring than a scar, I beheld merely the
same face wearing an unbecoming cap of closely knit curls
in place of my straight hair caught on the side by a barrette.
No matter how I twisted and turned, I remained myself,
unchanged. There had been no rite of passage after all.
What was to be expected of homemade coiffures? Miss
Nelly did not possess the art of a professional. Like a school
girl unprepared for college entrance examinations, her years

of house calls would, surely, disqualify her for any beauty salon. With a wet brush, I tugged furiously at Miss Nelly's handiwork, as though the tight curls had been a nest of coiled vipers. For the moment, even the thought of my black and white moonlight satin Pierrot costume had no power to console. It was, after all, only a slightly used item from a secondhand theatrical rental store.

As a bit player on a moving picture screen is seen briefly and not again, Miss Nelly was forgotten. Now a lifetime later, from an open bottle of shampoo she emerges. I hear again the discreet knock and the timid opening of my mother's bedroom door, as the hairdresser enters, carrying her black bag with the tools that once I had believed were endowed with the magic to promote me into the ease and grace of adulthood. For years, I had never wondered where Miss Nelly's home might be, or if she had any friends or relatives. Now, I ask myself whether her death, like her life, had passed all but unnoticed. In restitution in my mind's eye, I see her stretched out upon a medieval tomb—her body rigid, long, angular, sculpted in enduring stone.

II. FLORENCE O.

Through some circuitous succession, I am the owner of a photograph album that once belonged to my aunt, my mother's sister. The cover is missing but on the flyleaf, a woman, dead for many years and remembered chiefly as a querulous drugged invalid, wrote in purple ink, still un-faded: Summers 1889–1890. The snapshots show my mother's family and friends, all belonging to a well-to-do German-Jewish society from New York City. They vaca-tioned in Europe, fearing the anti-Semitism they might find at American resorts. In the pictures they are posed against indistinct backgrounds: an iron filigree hotel balcony in Paris, an Alpine meadow, a church, a foreign street with a passing, ghostly horse and carriage, a *Kurhaus* promenade. Each scene is labeled painstakingly in the same purple script, but I can barely recognize my mother's younger self nor her sisters nor some of their friends, while strangers may acquire familiarity, due to the repetition of their likenesses on the pages of the album. Miss Ogden, for instance, is she a paid companion or one of those chance acquaintances who, like a hot house plant, is forced into the early bloom of transient friendship common to Americans in Europe? An occasional male with a lavish mustache and stiff straw hat, might he be a candidate for suitor? I examine all the faces with avidity, as though by doing so I might deny the erasure of the years. But hindsight is a veil that distances me from those youthful countenances.

Only Florence O. appears ageless, hardly different from when I knew her during her childhood. She is no hot house flower, rather, a stunted *Bonsai* tree, for she will neither flourish nor grow, and her early aspect foreshadows her future as an old maid.

In the nineteenth century, the spinster was often a forceful presence: Balzac fashioned Cousine Bette into an evil, monolithic schemer, and just as New York City's high-stooped brownstones are preserved as nostalgic landmarks, the old-fashioned, unmarried ladies in the novels of Henry James and Edith Wharton retain for us today a lingering fragrance of attar of roses, while the multigenerational families, described by Tolstoy, would be incomplete without their aging female single relatives and retired nannies who carry heavy bunches of wardrobe keys at their waists, with the dignity of officers bearing their medals. The Victorian spinster was frequently the appointed caretaker of an old parent and although in life and fiction her lot was a dreary one, like a British son designated to serve the Empire, she had her necessary slot in society. But the old maids recalled from my past existed unanchored, a dying breed to be superceded by the single woman of today, who cannot be considered as even a remote descendant.

Florence O., although she was a lifelong friend of my mother's and welcome in our home, would always make a humble entrance there. Her uncertain mien clothed her like a shabby hand-me-down dress, ill-fitting and unbecoming, her cheerfulness was forced, and she seemed to be murmuring inaudibly to herself "everyone is so kind . . . but I know I'm not really wanted here . . ." To all eyes, she was stamped with the words, "old maid," more disfiguring than a pockmarked skin, though, in actuality, she was no homelier than many others. She had a round face, but it was slack, creased like a deflated pink balloon, and her shapeless body was precariously balanced on slender ankles and dainty feet that were her sole vanity. Her thinning hair was teased into a pompadour and it had a suspicious mahogany tinge. In those times, to admit to dyeing one's hair was as taboo as the mention of genitalia— male or female—even in the privacy of the bedroom. A rare artificial blond, brunette or redhead might be heard to exclaim: "White hair simply does not run in my family!"

But I believe that Florence O., having never moved forward, feared with even more violence than yesterday's *belles* the diminishing, blanching effects of time.

Her sister was scarcely more appealing than her sibling. Childless and living alone, she was, nevertheless, a divorcée, which, automatically, placed her in a superior category to Florence, who treated her with deference yet no apparent envy. The anodyne of habit had resigned Florence to her spinster's life, inevitable, and as much a part of her person as her name.

I used to wonder why bachelors, unlike old maids, commanded respect. A school friend of my father's, a Frenchman living in New York, without family, was a frequent guest at our Sunday lunches. Rendered speechless by a stroke, he was obliged to converse via pad and pencil, which he carried in the pocket of his dapper vest. Though pitied for his affliction, he appeared confident, even jolly. And I, for one, was fascinated by his dexterity that could transform a grotesque handicap into a magicianly parlor trick.

But Florence O. was merely an object of charity. How did she manage to fill her days without a man or children to cater to, no occupation? Did she merely wait for the afternoon tea hour when she would make those apologetic appearances into other people's homes? In winter, when I returned from school, I would often find her sitting cozily before the blazing coal grate in our living room while my mother poured from the ceremonial silver tea urn. But before the moment when the awaited sound of my father's latchkey would be heard at the front door, Florence scurried off, a mouse, to her secluded hole, grateful for the sip of domestic beverage and the crumbs of hospitality dispensed by a member of the privileged order of matrons.

Yesterday in Central Park, I had a chance encounter with a friend, an unmarried woman. It was spring, and she and the man she is living with, currently, had left their offices for an hour of jogging before dark. I watched her approach, a slim, youthful figure, despite middle age, attractive even in her gymnastic outfit. She waved, but would not pause to interrupt the rhythm of her trot. Soon, the couple in their identical red, white and blue exercise pants, T-shirts and Keds disappeared around a bend in the path, and I continued, in what seemed to me, now, a sedate pace. I marveled at the revolution that had taken place so quickly: The "old maid" had vanished like the dinosaur, but she has not been included in a brightly lighted showcase at the Museum of Natural History! Her kind may be found only in the hidden recesses of memory.

III. AUNT HARRIET: A FAIRY TALE ON UPPER BROADWAY

In today's papers and on television we learn of innovative scientific methods of reproduction: *in vitro* fertilization and sperm conservation, as well as many types of experimental sociological family units. These appear as contemporary phenomena—matter for news, indeed. Yet I recall a surrogate mother, a spinster parent whose case never reached the press. Her predicament had acquired, through the years, the surreal fatalism of a fairy tale, retold.

Once upon a time in New York City there lived a couple to whom Providence had granted everything— health, wealth and good looks. Only one thing was missing from their lives and they grieved each day over this omission: The blessing of parenthood had been denied them.

Far away, at the edge of a black forest, a poor farmer and his wife eked out a penurious existence from the soil. Fate had deprived them of all gracious things and, to make matters worse, the woman was big with child and the impecunious pair did not know how they would be able to feed another mouth.

In their Park Avenue apartment filled with costly bibelots—porcelains, Chinese screens, polished silver and tasseled damask draperies—the rich couple (Gabriella and Samuel) employed a battery of servants to cater to their needs. Through some miracle, contact was made with the farmer's wife and, in their dire need, she and her husband allowed their baby soon after birth to be spirited away into the empty, idle white arms of Gabriella. The infant was named Beatrice (which means happiness) and it was told that she was beautiful beyond compare—golden-tinted, rosy-cheeked, plump as a squab. For a while, the rich couple was contented but, in the way of their kind, they soon grew habituated to this latest blessing and longed greedily for more.

Meanwhile, the poor husband and his wife were still scratching a meager living from their small plot of unwilling soil and they agreed, in exchange for another stack of money, to make a second baby to order for the spoiled pair in New York. After the necessary time, another daughter was born and also duly dispatched across the country. She, too, was a lovely baby but not quite as dazzling as the first. It was as though her beauty had been filtered through clouds, while Beatrice had the full brightness of the sun on a clear day, and she remained the cynosure of all eyes. When she toddled from her nursery crammed with stuffed animals and tufted in pink silk to be displayed to guests for five minutes before bedtime, all the women envied Gabriella for being the possessor of such a priceless object, more glowing even than the gold and gems she had owned previously.

But just as a storm arises suddenly on a perfect summer's day, Gabriella and Samuel began to quarrel and they soon decided to part. Lawyers were summoned, dark-suited, stiff-collared; with cold words they divided the properties, the two baby girls included. And it was decreed that Beatrice would belong to Samuel, while the younger remained with Gabriella. The sisters were separated forever and furthermore, under no circumstance, would either sibling in the future have any contact with the parent that the law had decided was no longer hers.

As for the farmer and his wife, they were never heard from again. It is to be supposed that they continued to sew and weed their miserable square of land near the dark forest . . . and we may hope that Providence in its wisdom never granted them any further progeny!

Twice twelve months passed, punctuated by the four seasons, each with its different face, and Fate struck another blow. While Beatrice slept innocently in her bed, her father died suddenly as though felled by lightning. The little girl was sent to Samuel's ancient mother; toothless and blind, subsisting solely on fine white bread soaked in milk, she was never able to see the child blooming beneath her roof. Before long, the old grandmother succumbed also and the lawyers, in their dark suits and starched white collars, reconvened. What to do? After studying the family tree, only one sere leaf was to be found still clinging to the father's branch. She was Harriet, a spinster sister dwelling alone in spacious rooms in the Ansonia Hotel, an imitation French Renaissance chateau, located on upper Broadway. Like a bouquet of tearose buds, the triple orphaned child was delivered to the palace tower.

At this time Beatrice had a friend who lived across Central Park, the green boundary dividing East from West in New York City. Suitably attended, the children traveled back and forth on visits. The friend approached the Renaissance palace on Broadway with curiosity but not without certain trepidations. Aunt Harriet, the withered jailer, waited there, somber and thin as a charred bone, dressed severely in black. She attempted to dampen the flamboyance of Beatrice by putting her into prim shirtwaists and skirts well below her dimpled knees. But this convent-girl costume was to no avail against round rosy cheeks, golden ringlets and clear topaz eyes. After gazing at Beatrice, it was no wonder that the friend who had ordinary hair and skinny legs only wished for dolls endowed with blond curls and brown eyes. But it was Beatrice's teeth that were her most remarkable feature: "dazzling," "pearly"—none of these accepted adjectives fitted them. When her shapely, full lips parted in a smile, they were revealed like small, perfectly matched rows of white almonds, appearing more edible than fashioned for merely chewing. One might wonder why the friend was not envious of this surfeit of physical wonders. Perhaps this was because Beatrice, warm as the sun, like that orb, was oblivious to her natural splendours. And generous, agile as a healthy young animal herself, she genuinely admired and encouraged her friend's more stumbling efforts at skipping rope and roller skating; while, on her part, the friend invented all manner of seemingly clever plans to free Beatrice from the clutches of Aunt Harriet. It seemed as though this formidable guardian had nothing to do all day but sit behind the glass partition of her parlor, spying into her ward's bedroom, where the door was ordered left open so that every move might be monitored. Even in Central Park, that neutral territory, the friend could picture Aunt Harriet's face plastered against a window of the tall tower on Broadway—a Halloween witch, sallow, with black hair and a long bony nose, the flesh between the nostrils cleft as though from pressure by a dull knife—and she imagined the rays of Aunt Harriet's suspicious eyes seeking the children even in the wooded fastness of the Ramble. Sometimes, in daydreams, she fancied that it was Aunt Harriet who was the prisoner, locked inside her living room with the all-seeing glass partition focused upon herself, or remembering Hansel and Gretel, she hoped that she might fall into her own oven—or simply melt away until there was no more than a black ink spot on her prized Persian carpet.

When Beatrice was permitted to visit at her friend's home, she wept at leaving and begged not to be returned to the dreaded care of her guardian. But as womanhood approached, and even though the restraints grew more hysterical, she seemed to acquire new confidence.

"Don't have anything to do with boys. Never let one even touch your hand!" cawed the old maid.

But it was already too late. Beatrice had absorbed an earthy awareness as easily as a plant sucks moisture from the soil. She explained the "facts of life" to her friend who only half believed them.

In time, as often happens in large cities, the two girls drifted apart. The boundary of Central Park divided territories no longer inter-penetrated by their visitings. But people who listen to fairy tales will ask, "What happened next? What became of the princess in the tower?"

The ending is not recorded. However, for those who persist . . . One night, a rope of golden hair was flung from a window and the prince climbed up to rescue the beautiful prisoner . . .

"And did they live happily ever after?"

Who knows?

As for Aunt Harriet, she still haunts the area. Not far

from the tall turrets of the Ansonia Hotel, there is an asphalt island in the middle of a sea of cars. Here, each day at noon an old man appears with a paper bag filled with stale bread to feed the pigeons. They cluster about his feet, pecking greedily. A few paces off, a lone crow disdains the feast. What is its nourishment? Those who still remember Aunt Harriet know that this bird lives on bitter bile. The old maid has been transformed into a bunch of dusty feathers with a sharp beak and beady suspicious eyes. Witches never die.

Chapter Nine

VIRGINS

Popular artists of the French Revolution created monu-
ments and paintings of symbolic women to celebrate the
spirit of the times. Almost two centuries later, in the United
States, the society photographer embodied the sexual mores
of his day in portraits of brides from the urban, upper
bourgeoisie. This "girl," and I use the taboo word advisedly
because she is extinct, not to be confused with the young
woman of today, was motivated by the contradictory
dictates of Romance, Sex Appeal and Virginity. She cultivated a style of feminine beauty as outmoded to contemporary view as a collector's model of an early Rolls Royce.
We are able to recover her image only on cardboard—one,
representing all—the same wide, innocent eyes, painted
lips, like a small black heart in the fashionable camera's
chiaroscuro, and, long, shining hair curled to graze the
shoulders. And, just as an aspiring steeple is poised at the
summit of a church, the pretty head with its pointed tiara or
wreath of orange blossoms is set above the magnificence of
the wedding gown, encrusted with pearls and lace, its yards

of train artfully draped at the base of the picture in whirlpools and avenues of lustrous satin. A photograph, dated June, 1938, is now as historic as that other allegorical rendering, the eighteenth-century heroine, trailing her tattered tricolor banner.

Yet, whenever I hear the lilting, sophisticated, yearning melodies, the courtly lyrics of Cole Porter's songs, the photographic bride starts into animation and the virgin, composite and anachronistic, emerges, sprung from the frame of time.

I

Around the country club pool, Linda walks, self-consciously, on high, wedge heels, her long, shapely legs baked the color of caramel, every curve of breast, waist and thigh exhibited in a tight, one-piece shining white Lastex bathing suit. Thus armored, she is out to lure a certain male from the group lounging under a striped beach umbrella. Like so many sword points, she feels all eyes upon her, but she feigns indifference while she prays for victory. The blast of August sun is ammunition and the faint smell of chlorine exhaled by the pool is sweeter, more aphrodisiac than Chanel No.5. At last, she joins the cluster on the rectangle of artificial beach, no larger than a child's sandbox. At sixteen, Linda is nervously aware that these are "college men" and that she is a mere fledgling waiting to be asked for that important "date," the imprimatur of popularity. Soon, he rises to his giant height, and moving to the edge of the pool, arches his body, arms extended backwards, in preparation for a showy dive. A demi-god exulting in his power, he disappears into the turquoise depths, then, sinuous as a dolphin, rises to the surface and cuts through the water with sure, strong strokes. Although his face is submerged, the muscles of his shoulders, the reach of his long arms, the fin-like propulsion of his feet that cause a small commotion of waves, convey, somehow, that he is aware of Linda's rapt attention. Dripping, he hoists himself out of the pool and squats so close to her that she shivers voluptuously as the cool water dripping from him shocks her sun-warmed flesh.

Casually, he lights a cigarette, saying, "Hi," the syllable, more interrogation than exclamation.

Suspended between success and failure, her heart hammers. "Hi," she manages to respond, hoping she sounds sufficiently remote, preoccupied with other matters.

"Who can defrost 'Miss Frigidaire'?" he queries his cohorts. Provocation or contempt? . . . the seconds elongate, quiver like the drops of water falling from his manly chest tufted with black hairs.

Mutely, she implores some unnamed force. Now, let it happen, now. Despite the quasi-shade cast by the beach umbrella, the atmosphere is stifling, even the pink enamel polish on her nails seems to be melting in the heat and the tight Lastex bathing suit is more corset than armor.

"I have some sure telephone numbers. Let's plunder the city," one of the stags proposes.

"Count me out," he answers. "I am planning to have a chilly date with 'Miss Frigidaire' tonight!"

An invisible lens records the scene. Although features have been rubbed out, a red striped umbrella, the gleaming white of a bathing suit, sun-tanned limbs and the shrill artificial blue of a country club pool have been preserved in the untrue colors of an early auto-chrome.

II

With the arrival of autumn, just as migratory birds fly away from their summer perches, the sexes separate, going their various routes to segregated ivy-clad institutions of learning. But, at the Christmas holidays, when snow is in the air and lighted trees appear, along with holly wreaths, tinsel and glutted shop windows, the sexes reconvene. Now, at eighteen, the virgins are drawing near to marriage, their common goal. Dizzy with romantic expectations, they twirl in the lush aviaries of New York City's ballrooms. On the perimeter of the dance floor the males hover, penguins in stiff white shirt fronts and black tailcoats, poised to swoop upon the winged creatures in their gauzy finery. A light tap from a white-gloved hand transfers the female from one pair of arms to another: Popularity is bliss. But the life-span of the whirling species is brief. Soon it will fly into a new environment, outside these preserves that society has contrived.

After the ball, the taxi carrying Susan homeward is tantalizingly slow, almost stationary. It seems to be the skyline of Central Park South that is receding and the park lampposts follow in dignified march. Gaunt silhouettes, they distribute their narrow flares across the snow-powdered terrain, familiar to Susan since childhood. In the embrace of her escort, over his shoulder through the rear window of the cab, she catches fleeting, spectral glimpses: The Carousel, usually bright with gaudy painted steeds revolving to the tinny sounds of a cranked music box, is a dark silent spherical shape; inside, the wooden horses sleep; the Mall, her childhood meeting place, is as lifeless as the ruins of the Roman Forum, a mere hint at the hearsay of an ancient history; and the Casino in the Park rises on its mound of land, a pagan temple to Eros. Soon it will be demolished, to make room for a public playground where new generations of children will busy themselves among iron culverts, bars, and rings, innocent of the time when the idle rich occupied this spot at sunset and through the night, "fox-trotting" to the smooth music of Eddie Duchin's band. The Casino will be buried in Susan's memory, but, at the moment, there is neither future nor past, as she comes up for air out of a smothering hug, she is totally absorbed by the geography in microcosm, the ridges, declivities and hollows of her lover's ear.

It is three A.M. and at Susan's parents' apartment everyone has retired, but the "den" is open, and just like a plump, opulent Madam, hospitable and knowledgeable in the age-old gymnastics of sex, the brocade upholstered couch waits to receive the couple. Susan watches as her lover removes his glasses, preliminary foreplay that never palls: His blue eyes appear in startling nakedness without their habitual guards. Then, locked together, he and she fall upon the soft accommodating cushions of the sofa. They explore every part of one another's bodies in haste, as though an inch might evade their mutual clutchings and discoveries. The delicate tissue of her gown is rent, the work of many hours of prinking for the ball is destroyed: Makeup that had been applied with the care and expertise of an Oriental caligrapher is smudged and devoured by kisses. But, just as consummation is about to be attained, they halt with difficulty; the lovers separate, making futile attempts to right their persons, buttoning, straightening their clothes. Interrupted and thwarted, they cannot look directly at one another, and, to Susan, the sound of the front door closing is both pain and relief.

When she wakes at noon, she feasts in bed on daydreams of her lover. Every word and gesture is savored and, in recall, she sees his eyes again, bluer, even more seductive, denuded of his glasses. He is in all things: The slice of sky squeezed between the tops of adjacent apartment buildings, the bar of sunlight on the wall of her room, the song of the traffic. And since his presence is everywhere, she does not need to miss him. Yet, she will listen all day, if required—through eternity—for the telephone to ring.

III

The waiting room is not as Joan had anticipated: It is just like an ordinary doctor's office. She reviews the steps that had led her to this place, while observing her surroundings with distaste and some trepidation. The mousy gray, grass wallpaper, the institutional furnishings reminded her of the all-female college from which she graduated only a week earlier. With spring, engagement rings had suddenly appeared on the third fingers of the left hands; they were new, like the leaves on the trees and the classes held outdoors in the sunshine. They heralded a matriculation that eclipsed the lesser one about to take place on campus. Four years of study and the tentative advocacy, by the faculty, of future careers had been dissipated like passing wisps of clouds in a clear blue sky of June, the preordained month for weddings.

The amassing of the trousseau had been so time-

consuming that Joan had had little time to spare for her
fiancé. But the honeymoon would remedy that. Sheets and
table linens were stored in boxes, but soon, the lingerie, like
rambler roses, would cling softly to her body. The wedding
nightgown, chaste, yet slyly seductive, symbolized the
culmination of romance and would place a seal on its
everlastingness. On that night she will welcome the solemn,
joyous loss of virginity. Through time, as far back as the
chivalric age, a sibilant, invisible chorus cautioned wait until
marriage, preserve, deny, until the antique prohibition had
become as natural as instinct itself. Yet Joan considered
herself modern, a product of the post-Freudian era—not for
her the female secrecy, the evasions, the pretense that the
pleasures of sex were reserved mainly for males. All that was
of the past; she was able to identify with the pristine passion
of Natasha in *War and Peace*, while confessing that the
pragmatic social twitterings of the Bennett daughters in
Pride and Prejudice bored her, the satire seemed dated. Joan
could not recognize marriage as a contract; rather, it should
approach revelation! As the date drew nearer, however, in
her mind's eye she saw the wedding nightgown stained with
blood and she was nervous, fearing that she might prove
awkward and, just as an adolescent is ill at ease with her
body, neither child's nor adult's, she felt, simultaneously,
timid, naive and adventurous. She and her fiancé discussed
the possibility of a private nuptial rehearsal. Together, they
inspected sites—obscure inns where they would be unlikely
to meet anyone they knew. But the country hotels were
drab, inadequate to the magnitude of the event, and so they
either departed at once or merely dined in the shabby,
genteel restaurant surrounded by vacationing families on

holiday, with screaming infants strapped into borrowed high chairs, and lonely, single, aging men and women trying to look less pitiful than they were. Once, under an assumed name, they ventured as far as a bedroom, but the soiled spread and the suspicious expression of the proprietress drove them away. It was then that the thought of Hannah Stone occurred to Joan. She had heard that this champion of women and birth control leader performed the minor process of perforating the hymen, cleanly, without much discomfort, so that the membrane, at last devalued, should not interfere with a perfect union.

There was only one other woman in Hannah Stone's waiting room. And, just as someone traveling on bus or train may study a stranger never to be encountered again, Joan takes note of the mannish suit, the fedora hat from which disorderly strands of gray hair escape; no wedding ring, a bulky black satchel hand bag, filled, no doubt, with Women's Rights pamphlets, Joan thinks. She was probably a suffragette, survivor from another day, who, like an Indian chief turned tourist attraction on his own turf, is reduced to a mere object of curiosity. When Joan's name is called, she heads for the inner sanctum, with weak knees, nervous out of all proportion. Why—since the surgery is insignificant and the decision had been entirely her own? Hannah Stone wears an immaculate, starched medical smock and she sits behind a wide desk. Her face looks tired and seamed, but it still bears traces of former prettiness. She reminds Joan of her anthropology professor, causing her to feel embarrassed about this mission. But Hannah Stone is a woman of few words and soon Joan is upon the examining table, while this lady academician, masquerading as a physician, searches in a drawer for an instrument. Suddenly, Joan experiences an irrational longing for her reassuring, grandfatherly family doctor. She has the impulse to jump off the table, to flee—but it is too late. Hannah Stone is there, and in her small, tough hand, she holds, purposefully, a gleaming, silvery rod.

Now the bride stands ready in her ceremonial dress. While just as a worshipper genuflects reverently before an icon, the fitter, on her knees, with pins in her mouth, makes final adjustments to the extended train. As from a great height, the bride looks down, without regret, at the room of her girlhood that she is about to leave forever, and she waits, motionless, for her entrance cue. She is the image of an image, a mirror held up to the society photographer's wedding portrait. But the perfect stereotype of the virgin's face is modestly veiled, hiding it from her eager audience as she moves serenely down the aisle. Her eyes covered by a foam of white tulle, she is blind to all tomorrows.

Chapter Ten

FACTS OF LIFE

The invitation had read, "To meet Dr. Stuart Smith, who will show his movie on sex education, *How We Grow*." As I stepped out of the elevator I was met by a muffled roar from the other side of the closed door—the savage greeting of the cocktail party—at once repellent and exciting, familiar yet promising.

Inside, Dr. Smith sat in the center of a semicircle of people. All heads were turned in his direction, attentive, respectful, almost pious. My host steered me toward him, introduced us and left me with a small, chilled drink in my hand to the scrutiny of the doctor's unblinking gray eyes, unnaturally magnified by thick glasses, eyes that expressed intelligent, tolerant comprehension. I felt sure that it had been years since surprise or pleasure had flickered across their still surface.

"I have explained that this movie has been created specifically for the sex education of children," he said, "but it also has value for the present-day adult, in terms of. . . ."

I observed Dr. Smith as he spoke. He was slight and

gray—gray hair, skin and clothes. But his frail body contained a type of controlled energy that was electricity
without warmth. He sat lightly poised in his chair, like a
giant moth and when he rubbed his dry, brittle hands
together, it was like the meeting of insect wings. I almost
expected to see a fine gray white dust rise between his
fingers.

The discussion grew animated under his expert
guidance. New guests arrived and slipped into the widening
semicircle. At last Dr. Smith rose. "If we are all here now,
I would like to begin. Where is the younger generation?"

Our host disappeared, returning with a procession
of children of various preadolescent ages (his daughters and
the children of some of his guests). They stepped through
the ring of adults and squatted on the floor in front of the
screen. Conversation died down, and all eyes were now
focused on the heads of the children as they sat, for the
moment unusually quiet, expectant.

Somebody switched off the lights. The picture
appeared. Now and then the impersonal voice of Dr. Smith
added a comment from a darkened corner of the room,
while the impersonal voice of Dr. Smith issuing from the
screen, went on explaining, clarifying, answering.

I watched the movie attentively for a while, and
then my mind began to wander. I kept trying to remember
how I had first learned about sex.

We were on a channel boat between England and
France when my mother attempted to tell me the Facts of
Life. It was my first summer in Europe, and I must have
been about seven or eight years old. Why she chose that
time and that place, what led to her talk, I could no longer

remember. But I recalled the sickish rise and fall of the steely white-flecked water and the prickly sensation of a rope attached to a life preserver that I was playing with. I could still feel the wet air and taste the salt on my lips. My mother was patiently explaining the process of reproduction with the help of examples from plant and insect life. Every now and then she would pause to ask, "Is that clear? Do you understand?" I invariably assented, although my mind was a jumble of protest. It was all impossible!

When I was thirteen I visited my cousin in California. I no longer had as much time for the imaginative reflection about the grown-up world that had occupied me when I was young. Life had become more prosaic, and I was, at once, more unthinking and more fearless. My cousin, two years older than I, was already interested in the snaring of the male species. I followed her lead, not yet understanding, but admiring and imitating. I remember the morning we went alone to a department store in San Francisco and bought ourselves Empress Eugénie hats, in vogue at that time. May's was a brown derby with a limp yellow bird falling precariously over one eye, and mine, a navy tricorne with a white dove (complete with shining black beak and eyes) nestled in its brim. We felt exhilarated, and on the way home, we stopped at the five-and-ten and May bought me a Tangee lipstick—my first. I remember it was the color of orange marmalade and tasted like perfumed disinfectant. We were women of the world, and we hoped all the men in the street were staring at us with longing. But when we reached home, our parents, half laughing, half appalled, removed our new hats, and the Tangee was scrubbed from my lips until they burned. I wasn't permitted to use it again, but I kept it like a little silver cartridge lying at the bottom of my jewel box.

In preparation for becoming a woman, my parents had me take lessons in interpretive dancing. There were five girls in the class, all of us on the fluttering borderline between childhood and adolescence, and these lessons were supposed to give us enough physical poise to take the next step gracefully. So far, we were just muscle-sore. The stiffness would just be receding when Monday afternoon rolled around again. At the end of an hour's exertion in Martha Graham's studio, we stood with weak knees and tired backs in our leotards, waiting for Louis Horst (composer, accompanist and Martha Graham's music director) to play the dismissal chord on the piano. "Hold your heads proudly," Martha Graham would order. "Always look like the Winged Victory!" Then, with trembling legs, we ran back to the dressing room to change into our clothes and hurry through the darkening winter-damp streets, forgetting the Winged Victory in our longing for the indulgence of a hot bath.

Yet I always looked forward to Monday with a lift of spirit. I couldn't dance; the stretching, contractions and contorting on the dusty studio floor belonged more to the gymnasium than the stage. But Martha Graham belonged to the stage; more than that, she was dedicated. I felt it, although I couldn't define it. I admired it from my different world and humbly realized that she wouldn't be giving us dancing lessons if she hadn't needed the money. Artists were always poor; I had just read *Trilby*.

One February afternoon, arriving early, I dawdled up the stairs of the shabby house where Martha Graham lived and worked, trying to remember how I would feel when I came down an hour later, hugging the banister for support. The house always smelled of the aftermath of cooking, combined with the odd musty odor of old metallic costumes and grease paint. Dust was everywhere. It coated the tall wooden doors and ran along the dark corridors. At the top of the stairs, I overtook one of my classmates. I remember that her name was Flavia, that she was thin and pallid, avidly read *Idylls of the King*, was subject to fainting fits and colds and had to wear white socks to dance.

Martha Graham's bedroom was on our left, and we noticed today that the door was blown ajar. We peeped through the opening. She lay on her back in the center of the big bed, her long black hair spread in a circle on the pillow like the rays of a mysterious dark sun. Her eyes were closed, and her face looked shut, too, as if it held a secret. Louis Horst sat on the edge of the bed, his fat pinkish chest bulging out of his unbuttoned shirt, his suspenders hanging slack from his broad waist. He was bending over laboriously to tie his shoelace.

Flavia and I looked at each other guiltily and then hurried in silence to the dressing room. We sat on the familiar broken-down brown corduroy couch and stared through the high windows that opened to nothing—the blank wall opposite. Then we both began at once, "How can she?" "That old man!" "He's so fat!" "Isn't it awful?" I had heard the rumor that Martha Graham and Louis Horst were lovers, but I had staunchly refused to believe it. Now, disgust mingled with the thrilling anticipation of breaking the news to the others. Later, as we were all scrambling into our dancing costumes, a feeling of lonely disloyalty came over me. To what? Why? I didn't try to analyze it.

We were sitting, shivering slightly on the cold, bare floor, when Martha Graham and Louis Horst appeared. Today, instead of the plain dancing uniform, she wore a floating garment with red polka dots and her hair was tied back from her face in a scarlet ribbon. How often I had studied her face! And I always found something new; sometimes it belonged to a queen from ancient Egypt, sometimes the high cheekbones and hollows became a stark theatrical mask. Today, polka dots, white face, black hair strained back from the high, rounded forehead and full dark red lips made me thing of a tragic clown.

We all watched her in silence as she moved across the floor to shut a window. Horst sat at the piano idly playing chords. His jowls shook as his hand hit the keyboard. I looked away.

Martha Graham joined our circle on the floor. "Ready for the first exercise," she said. "Everyone is very quiet this afternoon."

Dutifully, we began. "One - and - stretch - and - bend - and -," she counted.

Whenever I could, I stared at her, thinking about what I had just seen, wondering about what I had just seen, wondering what she was thinking. Now with her draperies spread around her, her gentle abstracted expression, she reminded me of a beautiful convalescent.

At last she rose. "Stop the music, Louis. There's no spirit in them today." Then turning around to us, she asked, "Shall I dance for you, instead?"

We could barely assent. Such a gift had not been offered us before. We drew back to the clear floor and Louis Horst began to play a Chopin polonaise. I still hear it now with the same excitement.

At first I noticed many unrelated things: Through the studio window I discovered a few stubborn patches of snow in Central Park; in Martha Graham's movements I recognized the transformation of some of the angular exercises we had been doing. I studied her feet, square and strong, thick as a panther's paws, the soles already black from the grimy boards. Then all of a sudden, the music and the dance took possession of me, throbbing, visceral and forceful; they were one, and I was one with them—pausing and advancing, again and again—free of the earth, yet of the earth. In that moment I thought I understood the relationship of Martha Graham and Louis Horst. I no longer repudiated it. I exulted in it. It was part of something I had never understood until now. Something that I would know someday, be part of, too. All the small divinations of my childhood culminated in one divination. I comprehended, deeply.

When the music stopped, and Martha Graham subsided to the floor, breathing hard, it was almost like pain. I tried to hold on to what I had just found, but it eluded me. Later I would find it again. I had learned.

Dr. Smith's film had reached the last reel, *Preface to Parenthood*. With the help of his continued comment, how simple it all seemed, how unmysterious! These children would be intelligently instructed, but were they, perhaps in some obscure way, also being cheated? I thought again of the winding obscure detours of my growing up, the surprises often found along the way.

When the lights came on, we all blinked in the new glare. I was surprised to discover that the audience of children had almost vanished during the final part of the film. Only two or three remained from the original group.

We crowded to the back of the room to congratulate Dr. Smith. He stood quietly against the wall with a modest half smile on his lips, uncommunicative now, as if a little in awe of his own achievement. It was almost as though he had invented Sex.

"A triumph . . ." "Such a privilege to be part of . . ." "Thank you, you are to be congratulated." When at last I reached the doctor, I heard myself repeating the words spoken all around me. We shook hands briefly.

Outside in the hall I heard a pounding of horse's hooves accompanied by a crescendo of galloping music. In an anteroom near the door I found the children grouped in front of the television set. So this was where they had gone, deserting Dr. Smith's method of education. On the screen a lone cowboy mounted on a giant white stallion was chasing a band of desperados over a craggy mountain pass. Earth flew, shots rang out, and the children sat, shoulder to shoulder, motionless, their backs tense with excitement.

The 1950s are buried, now, also. On the television screen, cowboy weapons have been replaced by city handguns and the dispassionate, scientific voice of a Dr. Smith or Dr. Kinsey is overtaken by the raucous demonstrations of sexual politics and warnings about AIDS.

Chapter Eleven

IN THE SHADOW OF YOUNG GIRLS IN PINK

After many years, I see them a phalanx of three Valkyries in baggy Brooks Brothers sweaters, mid-calf skirts and flat-heeled rubber-soled saddle shoes, the standard wear for female college students in the late 1930s. Alice, Maggie, Edith—they would have been considered beauties in any era. Alice, a mid-Westerner, resembled a Gibson Girl, with long fair hair pulled up into an untidy chignon from which strands escaped in wavy trickles; Maggie, a New Yorker (her parents were wealthy patrons of music), was Jewish, her eyes were black and her smile was flashing and bold; Edith, who came from Glen Cove, Long Island, possessed the casual good looks of an F. Scott Fitzgerald prom idol. They were united by the Cause, their shared dedication to the utopian dream of the Russian Experiment. This vision permeated the campus of Sarah Lawrence College and universities throughout the country where the faculty influenced the students leftward, away from capitalist parents who paid the tuitions but were treated by their children with the condescension of missionaries among the heathen.

But unlike the other "radicals," Alice, Maggie and Edith were known to be activists. During the summer holidays, they did not revert to sun themselves around some country club pool by day and fox-trot at night but like the militant offspring of the god Wotan, they went forth, bravely. In Moscow, they met with workers and paraded across Red Square, undaunted by its vastness, barbaric colors, the cruel glint of its clustered onion domes and the fierce presiding hulk of the Kremlin. In the fall they returned to college as heroines who had participated in a movement in a foreign land that was as unreal and mythical to me as the Rainbow Bridge and storm clouds of Valhalla, framed by the proscenium arch of the stage at the Metropolitan Opera House.

Time and memory weave their spell, altering perspective. I can barely recognize a blurred, anonymous silhouette—myself—in those days while the fresco of three female warriors (virtually strangers to me; seniors when I was a freshman), is painted large in unfading colors upon the walls of the pseudo-Tudor buildings of a women's college campus in Bronxville, a meager commuter's distance from New York City.

When I sat in the basement library going through the motions of study, I dreamt of a certain "Yale man," the joys of the weekend just past and the prospect of the one to come. But I always looked up from my book at the entrance of Alice, Maggie or Edith on their purposeful way to the stacks devoted to Soviet Russia. Despite my insecurity and theoretical recoil from crowds and mass movements in general, there were moments when, just as a housewife may wish to try the role of femme fatale, I longed to be a joiner. And the sight of Alice, Maggie or Edith poised for an instant at the top of the library stairs appeared to my eyes like the statue of the *Victory of Samothrace*, in triplicate, fashioned in glowing flesh, draped in the flag of the Russian Revolution.

The small campus was limited to one steep hill with buildings, institutionally conventional in imitation of the traditional halls of Oxford and Cambridge, combined with the comforts and raw newness of suburban Bronxville. But one had only to enter a classroom to find oneself in a seething left-wing cell. The girls would be grouped informally around a table with the professor, at once "pal," psychologist and intellectual leader in their midst. The discussions were animated by the prevailing iconoclastic, "fellow traveler's" ideology rife in academia at that date. Since "English" was to be my major in my freshman year, I saw a great deal of the Greenwich Village poet, Horace Gregory. He was confined to a wheelchair by some incurable neurological disease which caused him to jerk and twitch and to speak in barks and gasps. But he had a febrile vitality and enthusiasm that converted the spastic movements of his upper body and his staccato utterances into exclamation marks peppering his inflammatory convictions. "We must examine these lines in terms of," (the latter phrase, an overworked expression of the day), "the socio-economic status of the day . . ."

Horace Gregory had lank, unruly, sandy hair that fell over his capacious forehead. The sharpness of his eyes was sheathed by steel-rimmed spectacles; his head was large, ill-matched with the fragility of his body, wasted by immobilization. His long fingers were stained yellow from a perpetual cigarette, which often slipped out of control, falling on the classroom floor where its burning tip resembled a miniature bomb. On the first day of college, after a one-on-one "don's" conference, a freshman from a reactionary "prep" school, unfamiliar with the intimacy between teacher and pupil fostered at Sarah Lawrence, announced, "Guess what? The old boy tried to make a pass at me!"

But it turned out to be merely Horace Gregory's habitual abrupt zig-zag lunge to recover a burning cigarette.

A lover, at once of the poetry of T. S. Eliot and the writings of Karl Marx, Horace Gregory contrived an amalgam of his two passions. We believed that Eliot's *The Waste Land* was a personalized Communist Manifesto, and, despite our freedom to argue, no one challenged this interpretation. It became as indelible as the nicotine stains on Horace Gregory's fingers, as accepted as his vehement barkings and his spasmodic gesticulations.

The majority of the faculty at Sarah Lawrence fueled the minds of its inexperienced, privileged students with zeal for a new social order. I was acquainted, however, with two important exceptions. The president of the college, Constance Warren, was a fossil left over from a young ladies' finishing school. Like a figurehead monarch with a liberal parliament, uncomprehending, yet indispensable, she pursued a calm, unaltered course among the firebrands over whom she ruled. While speaking another language, her ministers accepted her and even awarded her a modicum of respect. Not so the students, who were wary about being drawn back into the retrograde world of their parents. We felt impelled to mock Miss Warren, who was, in fact, a comic sight as she moved with dignified hauteur over the hilly confines of her realm. A spinster, tall and shapeless, wearing British tweeds, she had a calm, refined pinched face that was out of place on the podium at ceremonial gatherings at Sarah Lawrence College. During her addresses, I observed the three Valkyries who appeared deaf, their faces expressionless, while the majority of the assemblage had difficulty in suppressing derisive giggles. Introducing a guest speaker, Miss Warren cooed, "This is Doctor—, who has kindly consented to spend the night with me."

The explosion of laughter could not be muted by the vigorous applause that followed. Showing a visitor around the Arts building, when she came to the photography department, the president explained, ". . . and this is the dark room where the girls develop."

Anecdotes about her malapropisms multiplied. Real or apocryphal, they were handed down from class to class like silver trophies. Later, I was able to recapture the timbre of Miss Warren's voice, if not the content of her pronouncements, in the trilling elocution of Mrs. Eleanor Roosevelt.

Another faculty misfit was of a different order. Dr. Nickolas Kaltchas was a Greek professor of history, an older man, a scrupulous scholar who taught part-time because of his damaged health. He had been gassed in the First World War and, for some reason, separated from his kind, he had migrated to the United States, finding himself a somber blackbird among the flamboyant cardinals at Sarah Lawrence College. Despite the fact that there were only four of us in his class on the French Revolution, he was no "pal"-psychologist and remained formal and impersonal, with his pupils who listened instead of "participating."

Nickolas Kaltchas was swarthy, with black hair and a short black brush mustache; he might have appeared fierce, but for the kindly intelligence of his eyes. He had a square body and walked with a cane, which contributed to his old-world continental aura. He was never seen on campus after his classes and in my imagination he strolled along a boulevard of some middle European city. Through his teaching, I became immersed for as long as he lived in the study of the French Revolution. It seemed to me the blueprint for all revolutions, but I was never certain if my ardor stemmed only from the brilliance of Dr. Kaltchas' mind, or whether, feeling myself an outsider to the political zeitgeist on campus, like a defeated candidate who takes refuge in a minority party with opposing views, I fell under the spell of this exotic, skeptical scholar, unassimilated in his country of adoption, out of step in his place of work. Nickolas Kaltchas died during my junior year. My study of the French Revolution ended and my shock and grief over his sudden death, though sharp, was of short duration. Yet, when in my mind I go back to that campus, it is he who greets me; I see his Greek barber's mustache, his slightly listing gait, his cane. An obscure, alien teacher, he is alive in recall, while many of the faculty "stars" are now indistinct: Max Lerner, short, virile, pugnacious, left-wing journalist and political writer; Joseph Campbell, boyishly handsome, idiosyncratic curator and reviver of ancient myths; and William Schuman, a youthful instructor of music in those days. All deceased, now, in memory, their early selves are shrouded inside their own fame.

Scenes to be recaptured are often the insignificant ones, unremarked at the time of their occurrence. Today, I am able to cross the threshold of the music studio at the bottom of the hill, adjacent to the post office. There, I encounter that other, the shade of my eighteen-year-old self in the company of a few special friends grouped around a piano upon which one of us plays, each morning, the same composition by Brahms, a reiterated romantic prelude to the eager dash for the mail that is still being sorted. If I hear those measures today, I shiver with voluptuous expectation—in our baggy sweaters, mid-calf skirts and saddle shoes, we were harem ladies, each in thrall to an individual pasha who dominated us during the school week from the remove of a male campus. I can remember the number on my mailbox, its combination and position on the wall perforated with peepholes. And just as a fisherman experiences satisfaction when he feels that nip at the end of his line, I palpitated at the sight of a long envelope, stamped with a New Haven postmark, crammed into the space of a cubby hole.

Abrupt sounds may vibrate into the future: the telephone that announces a death, the noon siren (the very voice of a flawless summer sky), preceding the awaited call from a lover, the urgent wail of an ambulance. At college, a clanging through the dormitory halls in the small hours of the morning was a summons to a fire drill. Pale, puffy-eyed and dazed, caught without makeup, our hair still in nets and curlers, half asleep, we barely recognized one another in the pathetic stragglers who stumbled outside into the chilly, unfriendly dawn. Only Maggie, who lived in my "house" looked unchanged. In her long burgundy robe, in control, at this sickly hour she could have been the leader of a brigade. Her luxuriant dark curls had never met with crimpers and her face needed no aid from rouge or lipstick. When the drill was over, returned to my room, I avoided the mirror with its reflection of my sleep-stricken features, and in a sudden gesture of self-dissatisfaction, I tore off my pale blue net and the curlers that had been wound in place so carefully the night before.

During the final week of my freshman year, I spent hours in the basement library trying to finish an exposé of the American "robber barons" of the nineteenth-century. I wished that I had had at my disposal the indignation over their iniquities that I was certain Alice, Maggie or Edith would have generated. But just as a squirrel collects drab twigs and dry leaves to build his nest in the eaves, my notes were gathered from dull tomes, and, like the rodent's, my diligence was seasonal, predicated on the number of days remaining before the end of school. I nibbled at the end of my pen and stared, bored, around the library, a stuffy cage that prevented escape into the golden bath of spring sun outdoors. The campus had shed its winter aspect and the Tudor buildings seemed to be refreshing themselves in a frilly tide of budded bushes and the moist greenery of new grass.

My roommate and I were packing for the return home, she to Chicago; I, New York. From the window I had a view of Westlands, the main building on the campus, originally the residence of Sarah Lawrence (founder of the college). Unlike its Tudor neighbors, it was colonial with white columns and bay windows. The graduation cere-mony took place on the lawn in front of its rosy brick façade. In my mind's eye, I saw the location garlanded by young women, pretty as flowers, despite their black matriculation robes. This year, Alice had been chosen valedictorian, an earnest Gibson Girl, with her delicate tendrils of hair showing beneath the stiff tasseled mortarboard headgear, while Maggie and Edith stood nearby, sunflowers against a garden wall. When they removed their academic uniforms, would they assume the Valkyrie's armor, helmet and spear, to do battle against class inequality? In a shadow picture cast by the alternate light and shade beneath old elms, I imagined the graduating class (Alice, Maggie and Edith among them), bending their heads submissively to receive the next crowning—the wreath and veiling of the bride.

I never saw Alice and Maggie again. However, not long ago, a lifetime later, I met Edith at a party. I could not find the F. Scott Fitzgerald heroine in the gray-haired matron, mother of four and grandmother. But she did tell me with a remnant of her former fighting spirit that she was working as a lay psychologist in a children's clinic and that she had not yet been forced to retire despite her advanced age.

The playing cards of history are constantly being reshuffled: winner ace, loser ace, good king, king of evil. They come and go in the reorganization of another deal. Once there were three young female warriors who crossed my path briefly; anachronistic, today, their faith has been invalidated. Yet, their image is preserved in the storage house of my memory, where many of my own mistakes and some of my triumphs, as well, are lost; it is the things that we have never done, what we have not been, that taunt us into remembering.

Years after my graduation from Sarah Lawrence College, I attended a reading of *The Waste Land* by its author. T. S. Eliot was an imposing figure, high, stooped, his cheeks hollow and gray, his nose bony as a buttress, his eyes sunk deep in recesses, he resembled the ruin of a Gothic cathedral. At the melancholy sound of his voice, my former misunderstanding of *The Waste Land* was expunged. Here was no revolt, no depiction of the decay of capitalist society, but rather, the timeless lament of a genius, staring into the abyss of his own seared, overcivilized, aristocratic soul.

Chapter Twelve

ANGEL IN THE HOUSE

The word "mother," once charged with so much significance, has been robbed of personal import. My parent has been dead for over half a century, and just as family anecdotes, often repeated, hover between the hazy horizons of atavistic memory and invention, my mother—the woman, Alma—has faded into unreality. Yet, I am bound to her by genetic ties and empathy.

How can I coax her back from legend? I study pictures from the attic, and, although the old-fashioned apparel (a lace collar, beribboned hat, leg-of-mutton sleeves) looks "real," and the ink of the studio signature seems hardly dry, the image of my mother is no more than a lovely landscape visited long ago. In vain, I try to summon an idiosyncratic gesture, a manner of talking, laughing, a revealing act.

Then my eyes light upon a green-glass inkwell on my desk, an obsolete object I salvaged from the dissolution of the home of my childhood. It is empty now, and its silver lid has been missing for years but, a magic lantern, it is empowered to illumine the past and I am able to enter, in recall, those vanished rooms and find every piece of furniture intact, in its proper place, as well as household artifacts like those that accompanied the ancient Etruscans to their tombs. Here, in these rooms, among familiar objects, perhaps, I may locate my mother, the "angel in the house."

In the period following the First World War, luxury apartments were built with a foyer, a windowless area of wasted space. Inside the earliest example that I am able to remember, an English "pram" refuses to be dislodged from its station next to the front door. But, just like those puzzle illustrations in children's books in which a person is cunningly concealed in the branches of a tree or the silhouette of a mountain range, the carriage is empty, its infant passenger blotted out in the folds of a furry lap robe. At the handlebars, an anonymous nurse is missing also. It is she who belongs at that post, as I believe that my mother shrank away from the manipulation of curbs, each jarring of the cushioned pram registering along her nervous system like the first signs of a minor earthquake. Within this primal foyer, the perambulator reigns alone, portentous, magisterial and empty.

In the next apartment, the entrance hall was remarkable, chiefly for its floral-patterned English cretonne wall panels. To my child's view, the blooms assumed gigantic proportions, the russet petals of chrysanthemums, thick as swollen, contorted fingers, the stems and foliage jungle dense. Behind this magnified scrim, I glimpse my mother in the company of her interior decorator, whose henna hair matches the flowering decor. My mother was inordinately pleased with these wall hangings in our foyer. Although she possessed a highly developed intellect, charismatic social skills and a warm, sensitive, enthusiastic response to people, she felt unequal to decorating a home, relying on the support and expertise of a "professional." And, just as someone who lacks the credential of a college diploma may be gratified to find that she can expound upon the writings of an author, unfamiliar to a university professor, my mother basked in the admiration of her friends before the bold decorating coup that introduced our otherwise sober, conventional home. The furnishings in the foyer were scant as the walls were taken up mainly by doors leading to the living room, kitchen, library and bedrooms opening off of a long, dark corridor.

In my room, two objects represented my mother. A slender chain with three white enamel daisy pendants, conserved in a filigree casket next to my bed, was envoy from her girlhood to mine, and a long, knobby stocking that made its entrance at Christmas, bulging with miniature, carefully wrapped gifts. I found its overstuffed silhouette hanging at the foot of my bed in gray dawn. During the night, my mother had fastened it there, anchored by red ribbon and topped by sprigs of holly, while I pretended to sleep in order to preserve the lie of my outworn belief in Santa Claus. Despite the dark, I could see that my mother was wearing her old flannel wrapper, her hair, unpinned, fell in a braid down her back, just as it did on the Barnard College graduation photograph of her nineteen-year-old self. I had heard from her contemporaries about her abilities and the pleasure she derived, during those years, from the study of cool logic and theoretical ethics, and, today, I see the black-robed girl in the picture as a gentle judge, a Victorian Portia. The mother I knew still had the same wide-set eyes, the classical perfection of features, but the braid showing beneath the mortarboard had been blond, now it was graying and fine lines criss-crossed her white skin. Yet, just as the rings inside the bark of a tree denote the mounting years, without diminishing the generous bestowals of nature, the ageing of my mother did little to destroy the foundations of her beauty. My bedroom was my own chintz bower. My mother who respected children and avoided the role of authoritarian parent rarely intruded. I can scarcely remember the ritual goodnight kiss, but the motes of city sun from my windows (their panes made of a special healthful substance called Vita Glass—now obsolete) filtered into my room, even in winter, warm beneficial rays caressing as maternal embraces.

My mother's bedroom, on the contrary, could be invaded at any hour of the day. On my way to school, I would sprawl with my books on the twin bed next to hers, and deliver my small concerns into her ready ear. Sometimes, when I caught her unaware, my mother's expression seemed sad, but over her mobile face, shadows passed rapidly. Occasionally, I found the cook there ahead of me, taking the morning orders. Her formidable presence reversed roles, and it was my mother who was subordinated by this bully in a butcher's apron, with a pirate's bandanna wrapped around her sweating brow. Afterwards, dutifully, my mother would recite the grocer's list into the telephone.

". . . five pounds of granulated sugar, a box of corn starch . . . are your apples good today . . . ?" A lesson memorized, but not thoroughly understood.

In the afternoon, even if she were resting, my mother was eager to hear my news, to sympathize, applaud or express astonishment. I never asked myself how she had spent the intervening hours during my absence, confident that, on my return, I would find her where she belonged, at home.

But in that first apartment, dimmed by the years, I retain the picture of a closed door. Periodically, I was forbidden entrance to my mother's bedroom, only the family doctor and my father were admitted; and, without comprehension, I overheard the words, "nervous break-down." In retrospect, I recognize that old-fashioned malady, endemic to wealthy, idle women of that era. Have the careers and rousing dictums of today's feminist created antibodies against this malaise, or does it merely go by some other name? My mother always emerged from her bed-room, perhaps, a shade paler, a degree more anxious than before—yet, essentially, unchanged. Scrupulously, she resumed, without amendment, the domestic routines of her days.

The apartment child moves through the level, box-like rooms of home as though traveling among the hills and valleys of different lands, each with its own topography, climate, produce and culture. The library was my mother's most-favored nation. Here, too, I was happy, free to roam at will. She sat at her English, eighteenth-century writing table, with its stationery-store collection of pens, pencils, clips, erasers, pads, writing paper, blotter, pen knife and magnifying glass. Later, a typewriter made its appearance and I see her with spectacles on the end of her nose, practicing her self-taught "hunt-and-peck" system. But the two most valued possessions were a worn leather portfolio containing private papers (that object, even the word itself, has become extinct, its meaning attached to high finance or diplomacy, its forms replaced by files, computers and word processors), and the green-glass inkwell presented to her by my father on their London honeymoon. It was her choice, as I am certain, he would have preferred a jewel for his bride. To this day, the sight of my mother's handwriting is, for me, her most intimate memorial. The library was a narrow room, but the books there expanded its walls beyond limit. A giant glass-fronted bookcase housed classics by Shakespeare, Homer, Virgil, Dante, and Victorian favorites: the works of J. M. Barrie, G. B. Shaw, George Meredith, Matthew Arnold, John Galsworthy, Arnold Bennett, Thomas Carlyle and Alfred Tennyson. The shelves on the facing wall held contemporary fare and a scattering of perennials for children: fairy tales by the brothers Grimm and Hans Christian Andersen, *Peter Pan*, *Peter in Kensington Gardens*, *The Wind in the Willows* and *A Child's Garden of Verses* by Robert Louis Stevenson. British authors were predominant in accordance with current Anglophilism. But it was *Alice in Wonderland and Through the Looking Glass* who reigned supreme. This young lady, polite, domesticated yet chronically anxious, surrounded by an unreliable world populated by monsters at once threatening, nonsensical and endearing, appears to me, now, as a stand-in for my mother—her conscientiousness, intelligence, her humor and her terrors,

> . . . either the well was very deep or she fell very slowly, for she had plenty of time as she went down to look about her, and

to wonder what was going to happen next. First she tried to look down and make out what she was coming to, but it was too dark to see anything; then she looked at the sides of the well, and noticed that they were filled with bookshelves; here and there she saw maps and pictures upon pegs. She took down a jar from one of the shelves as she passed; it was labeled, Orange Marmalade, but to her great disappointment, it was empty; she did not like to drop the jar for fear of killing somebody, so managed to put it in one of the cupboards as she fell past . . .

Lewis Carroll, *Alice in Wonderland*

I would sit quietly while my mother read aloud to me from the red, gold, embossed volumes inscribed. "To Alma, on her tenth birthday, from her loving Papa. March 12, 1882.

I did not understand, altogether, the tales, but during these hours I felt very close to my mother, as though we were of one age and she were confiding in me. The red and gold books have been permanently mislaid, and they will always be exclusively my mother's property, but the image of Alice carried into other editions is closer to me than any family portrait.

As I grew up, I sensed that certain books in the library afforded my mother greater companionship than her long-lasting, flesh and blood friendships. Today, I can place these writings in a single category, and I am able to find the reason for their disproportionate contribution to my mother's life. Now, they share the label "Women Writers," but as an adolescent, I read them enthusiastically, while overlooking any overt or tacit message—George Eliot, Virginia Woolf, Elizabeth Bowen, Katherine Mansfield, and the letters of Jane Walsh Carlyle, whose clever mind was subdued by the thunderous prophesis of Thomas Carlyle, her cantankerous genius husband. Individually and in concert, victim or rebel, they spoke to the intellect and heart of my mother, who was both fortunate and deprived, grateful and frustrated, untried in the world outside the protective cage of her home. She lacked the distance, and, perhaps, the courage to rupture the constrictions imposed by her gender, class and era, and, like someone starving in the midst of plenty, she turned, hungrily, to the company of her reading.

The kitchen was off-bounds, penetrated, only rarely. This large, dark steamy realm, belonged to the bandanna-crowned cook. Enroute to visits to Bini's room, I glimpsed this tyrant standing before the monstrous, old-fashioned, hooded stove. The sole window in the kitchen faced a shaft and perpetual night held sway, but the odors issuing from the ungainly dinosaur range were enticing, satisfying as the actual consumption of a meal. A whiff from a juicy roast or luscious chocolate soufflé can transport me back in time and across the national borders of my childhood home to that kitchen. My mother who read the epics of Homer and Virgil in the original Greek and Latin and spoke fluently three other foreign languages was as ignorant and helpless as an infant when she passed this threshold. It is my belief that she never cooked an egg nor even boiled a pot of water, and just as a tourist may regard the immensity of the Sphinx, she approached the stove with uncomprehending awe. And, amazingly, she was also incapable of thoroughly tasting the dishes when all those promising odors materialized on our dining room table. As in the folk tales in which fairy godmothers shower upon an individual at birth every gift, save one, my mother had been born without a sense of smell. Her delicate nostrils were, in the main, ornamental. I found this incredible and performed verifying experiments: My mother's preference for simple nursery food was one proof. She enjoyed ordinary ginger-snaps and anaemic vanilla ice cream—the first, sharp and stinging, the second merely cold and bland, both depending on sensation rather than taste which is the counterpart of smell—epicurean siblings unable to thrive without one another. For my mother and me, the remote region of the kitchen would always remain interdicted territory where a witch stirred her boiling cauldrons at the very center of our otherwise ordinary home.

The living room—it should be called "parlor" because of its stiffness and because no one ever "lived" there. In memory, it appears unoccupied and I have difficulty in placing my mother among the dark gray brocade sofas and pleated silk lampshades. A tall, English mahogany secretary was never opened and just like a dignified, tight-lipped guest, it surveyed the room and, especially, Madam Dessoff's spindling bowlegged Louis XV chairs, with disdain. Fleetingly, my mother shows up seated at her piano, and among the shifting lantern slides of recall, her face is reflected, distorted, against the polished sides of a silver urn, belonging to an heirloom tea service as she pours for a friend, before the hot flame in a charcoal grate, at five o'clock on a winter's afternoon. The parlor belonged less to my living, immediate family than to the stern portraits of my maternal grandparents on the wall flanking the mantle. I never knew them but the paintings, just like chaperones on the sidelines, seemed to be disapproving of the next generation, reproaching my mother, and me, the product of my *laissez-faire* upbringing. My grandfather was portly, pompous and he sported a flourishing handlebar mustache. My mother had inherited his broad brow and thoughtful gray eyes. Her mother had bequeathed beauty. In the portrait she was a matronly ex-belle—a brunette, she wore a tightly curled bang that resembled black lace, and the bovine expression of her hazel eyes was contradicted by the firmness of her chin above the high collar of her dark velvet dress. A red rose pinned to her ample bosom was an added fashionable note. Although, recently, the painted pair perished in a fire, in a far corner of my mind they still survive, the hosts of that tenebrous, unlived-in living room.

One afternoon, just before my marriage, I returned home to find the library strewn with a storm of linen. I existed at that time in a state of self-absorbed oblivion brought on by romantic love and the busyness of wedding preparations, not even the ugly threats from Europe were able to reach me. Yet, that day, I took note of change in my mother, who, like an angry angel appearing out of thick, creamy Michelangelo linen clouds, announced: "Look at these! Your mother-in-law-to-be saw fit to have them sent here; she evidently doesn't believe that I am capable of choosing your trousseau!"

The linens had arrived unsolicited, despite our own exhausting hours of shopping. My mother's fury was uncharacteristic, incomprehensible. The blue veins that marbled her white temples stood out, throbbing, engorged as snakes, and she seemed to be strangling on ropes of smooth bed sheets. The scene had the grotesque unreality of a dream, but suddenly her mood altered. Her habitual anxiety returning, she said, "Call it off. You are not ready for marriage. Learn to stand on your own feet first. Use your mind to strike out for yourself. I never did, no doubt my fault, but I had no one to warn me. Profit from my mistakes."

It was a strange plea to be addressed by a mother to her joyous daughter on the eve of marriage.

Now, long after, as in the crystal ball of a fortune teller, I read the signs of a past foretold. My mother was unable to tolerate the well-meant interference of a confident, practical, worldly woman because it revealed to her that, despite her efforts, she had always been a misfit inside her home, the prisoner of mores. "Wait," she repeated, "I have every confidence in you. Earn some confidence in yourself before—"

With the positiveness of inexperience, I interrupted her, "Speak for yourself! I am different from you—and I know what I want!"

Together, in silence, we folded the tablecloths, napkins, towels and sheets into their boxes, to be returned to the source. A petty revenge had been achieved.

YESTERDAY

Chapter Thirteen

THE VAMP

Woman's role is dominant today in our thoughts and actions, and, despite compromises (an unjustly disparaging word), we are moving in the right direction. But just as an evangelical mission in its zeal creates a single stereotype from the misguided primitive beliefs of an entire population, current propaganda tends to regard yesterday's female exclusively as victim, the passive property of the male sex. Yet, the kitten, a domestic pet, and the tiger belong to one genus; the "angel in the house" and the vamp were both women. The latter, a wily expert who snared the besotted male for the furtherance of her own goals, money and social power, is largely forgotten and often confused with her lightweight sister, the flirt, whose chief aim is merely to please the opposite sex. Just like the butterfly, she still hovers, here and there, in the hostile environment of feminist pesticides, but the vamp has become an extinct species. She may be studied in Victorian literature—Thackeray has made her central in his novel, *Vanity Fair*—and she is vivid, while the sweet child-brides of Dickens fade, even as we read their stories.

I was acquainted with one flesh-and-blood specimen of the order of vamp. And, as Olga X was, also, a Russian emigrée, her twilight aura was composed of the aftermath of two setting suns. A certain shade of turquoise blue, whether found in a jewel, a piece of cloth, a patch of sky or the broken shell of a robin's egg, recalls her to me: her deliberate malapropisms, her quaint mispronunciations of the English language, her tawny skin, slanted golden eyes, her golden hair, prominent, Tatar cheekbones, with a coquettish black mole on the left side. And, just as a logo sells merchandise, Olga, a vamp, used her hourglass form, swathed in that special, delectable, not-to-be-forgotten shade of blue, for her own promotion.

Biographical notes on Olga's early life are scant, consisting of scraps related by Ben, her American husband. She was always remarkably silent on the subject of her past. So her history remains haphazard, depending on the subjective views of one interested party, then relayed to me, second hand. Furthermore, the fate of a single individual is dwarfed, played out, as it was, against the gigantism of the Russian Revolution.

Like all aging beauties, Olga was evasive about the date of her birth, but by a system of approximate arithmetic, I deduce the year to have been 1904, in a suburb of St. Petersburg, where her father, a Russian noble, was the owner of a factory. Her mother, a Yugoslavian actress, ran off soon after Olga's birth and was not seen again. Olga, an only child, was reared by her paternal grandmother and her father. Although she never knew her mother, she showed

me, proudly, a photograph of her: Pretty in the baby-faced
fashion of a silent movie starlet, she was wearing a Turkish
turban and in no way did the immature image resemble
Olga's sharply defined features. Concerning Olga's education and friends, I learned nothing. But out of that blurry
past, I hear the report of gunshot. It represents the Revolution in microcosm, for Olga's father has been assassinated
at the factory by his own workers, and on the momentum
of a bullet, Olga and her grandmother flee to St. Petersburg.

At this juncture, there are blank pages in the
biography. But from my reading of Tolstoy, I set the scene,
to be revised after my visit to Leningrad a few years ago. As
in a dream, in which the familiar is distorted, unrecognizable, I looked, in vain, for the city of Anna Karenina, the
troikas and the balls, but found, instead, the map of streets
followed by the student, Rasholnikov, in his attempted
escape from justice, in Dostoevsky's *Crime and Punishment*.
The Imperial Palace is a museum, although the retaining
walls of the mansions of the aristocrats remain, the interiors
have been gutted, converted into apartment cells, the
bronze equestrian statue stands, frozen, overlooking the
frozen Neva. Rococo, Italianate buildings, painted in pastel
colors line the Nevsky Boulevard, they look as trivial as
sugar icing on a birthday cake next to the immensity of the
avenue, deserted in January's cold. Everywhere, there are
the distorted perspectives of Saul Steinberg drawings.

What became of Olga during the destruction of St.
Petersburg and the rise of Leningrad? I heard from Ben that
she had been employed by a drafting firm, or that she
danced with the Bolshoi Ballet, but she had not been
trained in any skill, her beauty was her only credential.

Perhaps, a fledgling Mata Hari, she might have extracted secret formulas from the American technocrats swarming Russia in the 1920s. One knows nothing for certain, except that she married Ben who had been sent abroad by the Dupont Company. For nine years, they continued to live in Leningrad, while Olga fantasized about the United States and its proverbial gold-paved streets, where every American businessman was a millionaire, her husband, included.

"And can you imagine after I arrived I found my 'personality' [another malapropism for 'myself'] on a filthy street in Brooklyn!" she told me years later.

Before that, Ben had made several abortive attempts to smuggle his wife out of Russia. They had even served terms in separate jails.

"Mine was not at all so bad. The clientele was mostly aristocrats," she said.

Here the biography picks up data with the details of Ben's successful maneuver to export Olga, concealed under a tarpaulin on a sailboat crossing the Black Sea to Turkey, where he and freedom awaited her. But, as long as I knew her, she was a prisoner. The shock of disillusionment in the United States during the Depression and the abandonments and violent uprootings that she had undergone were traumas that made it impossible for her to move from her modest apartment in southern Connecticut—even when Ben was able to offer her another, grander home. For Olga, any change had become a passport to the terrors of dislocation.

The condominium in Stamford was an altogether American product, but on entering Olga's apartment you were in old Russia. The living room was crammed with bibelots of all kinds, including china statuettes of shepard-esses and sleek, voluptuous female nudes that reminded me of the plaster nymphs and goddesses that lined the halls of our dilapidated antique hotel in Leningrad, where fat female wardens were posted at intervals to dispense exit and entrance passes to tourists. Olga's furniture was painted white with gold trim, upholstered in velvet and satin, heavy, opulent drapes and swags at the windows smothered the view of her rose garden and Long Island Sound, dotted with sails. A grand piano and a tall, haughty, golden harp dominated the salon. Although Olga no longer played any musical instrument, she kept these pieces as essentials for an affluent, cultured atmosphere.

Outside her own walls, Olga might suffer uneasi-ness, but within her small kingdom she reigned over her possessions, quarreled with her husband (a subjugated Prime Minister), persecuted every speck of dust and cut her rosebushes back to size with the violent self-assurance of a mini-Catherine the Great.

Sensing how long the days of her captivity must seem and admiring her exotic costumes, designed and sewed by herself, I asked if she had ever thought of applying her talent to some professional venture.

"Vat!" she exclaimed, and her nose seemed to grow sharp as a stiletto, her golden eyes, angry as a tigress, "Vy should I vork to make other vomen beautiful?"

A virtual recluse, who had outlived any concern with men, she distrusted women and scorned her middle-class neighbor couples; yet just as the idle piano and harp were polished and tuned, she maintained the perfection of her features: The mauve pink of her heart-shaped lips, the mascara on the lashes of her slanted, Slavic eyes and the gold of her hair, teased into a high pompadour, they were the components of a show without audience.

So it was a surprise to receive from Olga an invitation to a country club dance. She usually avoided the premises and the members who were forever playing games—golf, tennis or bridge—and damaging their skin by lying in the sun next to the crowded pool, agitated by the splashings and duckings of overactive children. The clubhouse was a fieldstone building with cheerful royal blue shutters. Inside, large basins were filled with seasonal flowers and the lounges imitated a spacious country home. But the tread of the golfers' shoes was heavy and the knobby knees and muscular legs of the tennis players of both sexes, in shorts, disgusted Olga. She entered the club only to avoid cooking at home, although her apartment boasted a separate dining room hung with a crystal chandelier. In the drawers of her Louis XV sideboard, her heavy, embossed nineteenth-century silver was neatly arranged and a matching cupboard was filled with china, multi-colored as the Russian Easter eggs hand-painted by Olga, the best specimens preserved from season to season and used as centerpiece for the unemployed dining room table. She and Ben habitually ate in the modern kitchen, and, although Olga could subsist on grapes and pickles, Ben's appetite was demanding and gross.

The night of the dance, she was truly resplendent in turquoise satin. Despite puffs and the suggestion of a bustle, the ballgown revealed the curves of her body and her tiny "vaist," that still measured only eighteen inches around, the cleavage of her bosom and her smooth, tawny shoulders dazzingly displayed by the deep *décolleté*. And just as a forest pond is tinted green, the diamonds in her ears gave off phosphorescent rays highlighted in turquoise blue from the surrounding satin yards of Olga's signature color. Next to her, all the other women were frumps and their paunchy, red-faced husbands, looking choked and apoplectic in their summer tuxedos, clustered around this rara avis who had strayed into their community, a peacock among barnyard fowl.

When the orchestra played its final number, the nostalgic *Blue Danube Waltz*, a group of men left the dance floor to surround Olga, who had removed one of her turquoise satin shoes and was filling it from a bottle of Champagne. She passed this loving cup among the thirsting maws and the suitors jostled one another in their eagerness to sip the aphrodisiac potion. The ceremony ended, she replaced the damp shoe on her foot and blew a farewell kiss at her admirers. And, just as a vestigal part of the body—an appendix, wisdom tooth or the leftover stump of a tail, located internally, at the base of the spine, though nullified by evolution, may outlast biological need—the instincts of the vamp endured in Olga after their usefulness had become obsolete.

I enjoy wandering in the subterranean depths of the basement of the Metropolitan Museum of Art, where the costume exhibits are mounted. In this morgue of fashions from past eras, the Napoleonic, the Victorian, the 1920s of the flapper, the faces of the dead are wiped out. They are replaced by blank, ovoid heads that remind me of the white celluloid darning egg used by our French maid to darn the heels of my mother's stockings. The Czarist display imported from Soviet Russia was the most splendid of all. In the airless museum underground, a *troika* and its cloaked passengers brought the frostiness of Russian winters. The toilettes, in their showcases, ranged from morning attire to full evening and ceremonial court dress; guardsmen, in scarlet uniform with gold braid and epaulette; and small children, miniature duplicates of their elders. Behind glass, diamond tiaras still sparkled and jeweled dueling swords looked ready to spring into action. Here I was able to recover some of the lost, adolescent efflorescence of Natasha Rostov from Tolstoy's *War and Peace*; there, I felt the presence of Anna Karenina that had evaded me on my visit to Leningrad.

Two female mannequins in equestrian habits stood side by side sharing a single showcase. Their long riding skirts lifted at one side revealed a glimpse of petticoat beneath. A segment of turquoise blue ruffle caught my eye. It gave me pause and I groped for something buried in memory. Now, as I walked around the exhibition, beneath the theatrical, anti-natural lights reflecting off black walls and ceilings, I was blind to the display, as I searched, within, for that object hidden by layers of forgetfulness. What was it that was nudging me for recognition? I had never been horseback riding in a Russian forest dappled with white birch trees; might I have encountered those equestrians during the long, lazy hours of some summer afternoon on the page of a novel? I returned to the double figures in the showcase on a hunt that had no predetermined quarry. The dark fitted, jacket and long skirt, the boots could tell me nothing. But, this time, at the sight of a turquoise blue flounce, the ovoid head of the dummy assumed features and color—golden, Slavic eyes, prominent Tatar cheekbones, coy black mole—they belonged to Olga X. I had given her no thought for years, but now I heard her voice, the histrionic foreign accent, saying in reference to her twin rider, "My 'vaist' is smaller than hers."

Chapter Fourteen

DEMONS AND SUPERNATURAL PRESENCES

The supernatural has been overtaken largely by the forces of the subconscious. "Good" and "Evil" have become "Sick" and "Well," but I knew, once, a demon. He crossed my path, a slender streak of fire and ice; I shall not see his like again.

There is a certain street corner, a sidewalk cafe, a special table with a particular view on the Quai Voltaire in Paris that, just as a monument commemorates a patriot, brings back to me the Polish writer, Jerzy Kosinski. Before the hour of our meeting, that location had been no more than an empty stage set, awaiting the appearance of the leading actor.

Paris is divided in two by the Seine, and as you sit at the Café Quai Voltaire, in front of you, across the river, you look at the Right Bank: the dignified government buildings, the Louvre in the formal paths of the Tuileries Gardens and beyond, the arcades of the Rue de Rivoli. This elegant cityscape is haunted by the shades of the *bel époque*: the *nouveaux riches* on display in their grand *équipages* or strolling among the geometric flower beds in the park, the ladies in long, rustling skirts carrying parasols, the gentlemen, high-hatted, in swallowtail coats. At your back, that maze of streets is the Left Bank, where you might fancy that the priest, whose cassock sweeps the dusty cobblestones, has stepped out of the Middle Ages. Here the ancient houses huddle, shabby and somber, mourning for their aristocratic tenants beheaded in the Revolution. A peoples' market, frequented by students and artists, permeates the atmosphere with the odors of vegetables and fruits. Adjacent to the café, there is a small hotel, where Oscar Wilde languished in inquisitorial banishment. The frontage sleeps; I have seen no guest going in or out, and the filigree balconies resemble the inscriptions on a headstone. To your right, the flow of the Seine leads you towards the sturdy twin towers of Nôtre-Dame, joining the two continents of Paris more surely than the spans of its many bridges. But if you draw close to the cathedral, its bastion contours are obscured in a welter of stone gargoyles—all manner of supernatural shapes—that seems to be saying Right Bank, Left Bank, are one; and evil lurks in cities, the creations of man.

On a fair spring afternoon in the 1960s, my husband and I were resting at the Café Quai Voltaire from one of those long, aimless rambles irresistible to the traveler in Paris. I was content to sit indefinitely at the white-clothed table just watching the pedestrians passing by. Suddenly, as though at command from an invisible director, the film blurred, the crowd seemed to go into slow motion and a single figure emerged, highlighted. When this stranger stopped at our table, I felt no surprise; the encounter had happened before—perhaps, in another existence. It was a déjà vu in the city of déjà vus. Where had I seen that swarthy face, with its hawk-like nose, the crest of hair, luxuriant and glossy as a raven's plumage springing from a peak on the low, broad forehead, the heavy black eyebrows, the small pointed ears, that body, thin as a razor blade, moving gracefully, lightly, as though in defiance of gravity? Was he the embodiment of a folk tale: a mischievous demon who stole the souls of pure village maidens and tweaked the noses of pious scholars bowing over their religious tomes? He might be the son of a king, transformed by a magic spell into a gypsy wayfarer. And I felt that, just as lightning splits an unchanging sky, this presence was empowered to disperse the placid, prudent, smug beliefs of the common sensical quotidian.

Yet he said, only, "How nice to see you. May I sit down?" His accent was faintly foreign, his words, staccato, issuing like ice pellets from his narrow lips.

My husband had known Jerzy Kosinski in New York City, and now he told us that he was about to return there for the publication of his first novel, *The Painted Bird*. The conversation that afternoon was unremarkable, but when he fixed his glance on me, with his wide-set black eyes, burning as coals, and commented, "I like your witch's hat," it was as though he were admitting me into a charmed circle. Although I had no idea, then or now, what this occult order might be, I conserved the black leather hat until it fell apart, its tall crown collapsed, its brim grown shapeless and frayed.

As soon as it was issued, I read *The Painted Bird*, and, for all the time I knew him, Kosinski was defined by this book. It recounts the experience of an eight-year-old boy, let loose, alone, in the forest, fleeing the Nazis. He came from a wealthy, upper-middle-class home, privileged with books, toys, a nanny and cultured parents, but from the first pages the child is presented as a wild gypsy, whose dramatic dark coloring makes him easy prey for his blond, Nordic predators. The narrative tells of his wanderings and his miraculous escapes during the war years. He seeks asylum in huts and farms and, everywhere, he is exposed to murder, rape, sadism, sodomy, incest and the spells of half human peasant crones. The small protagonist is wily, agile and resourceful, he has the courage of those unacquainted with self-pity. A sprite, he manages to survive and terror renders him strong as an army of one. He is oddly detached from the suffering of human beings, his pity is, chiefly, for animals who accept their hideous fates with dumb stoicism. The death of a single cart horse brings tears to the reader's eyes, while the corpses of men and women are cause for nausea and shock. Armed with his "comet," a type of lantern used as seeing eye, stove, body warmer and amulet, the boy lives, at intervals, in the woods. In winter he glides over the ice with the help of a handmade contraption, part skates, part sail. He binds himself in rags against the cold. In summer, he feels close to the small creatures of the forest, and somehow manages to evade the fangs of the wolves. His rapport with nature is spontaneous, unpoetical, difficult to explain in a pampered city child, but it is never doubted. Magic has its own reasons, unsuspected by the rationale of the psychologist. At the close of the book, at the war's end, the boy is befriended, temporarily adopted by a unit of Russian occupation soldiers, but the dark-painted bird is still isolated from the flock, his loneness is now reinforced by silence, for trauma has made him mute.

The Painted Bird is unique in the literature of the Holocaust, arousing shudders more than empathy. Hell is not to be depicted in humanistic terms. Of course, the tiresome cliché arises: Is it autobiography or fiction? *The Painted Bird* is fantastic as the grotesques in a painting by Hieronymus Bosch painfully real as cautery.

This work and a second novel, *Steps*, made Jerzy Kosinski a celebrity. He could be seen at New York City's literary gatherings, still outstanding, as though his fellow writers and acquaintances had cut a swath around him. Urbane, impeccable, he wore smartly tailored, made-to-order suits, pinched here, flared there, to accentuate his swaggering grace. Although his height was average, his glossy black head, with waves of hair clustering around his pointed ears, and his swarthy sardonic face seemed to top the company. He was difficult to know, and just as a performer is concealed by his roles, Kosinski was elusive through many guises and his tall tales of pursuit, international espionage and torture. By turn, he had been impoverished, homeless, or rich, with an apartment in every city of Europe complete with a duplicate wardrobe so that he could take off free of baggage at a moment's notice. He played polo and skied with the jet set; hob-nobbed, disguised as a professor, with academics in secluded quadrangles; wandered, alone, at dawn, through slum streets and along docksides festering with vice.

He described to me several versions of his whirlwind courtship of the young widow of a millionaire Pittsburgh industrialist. The contact had been made soon after Kosinski, a penniless emigré, had arrived from Russia through his right-wing books on economics, written under the pseudonym Joseph Novak. The marriage was of short duration.

"We were an ill-matched pair," he had mused. Yet when she died, he mourned and during her final illness, though divorced, he recalled that he lay on the floor outside her hospital room, "like a dog."

Was he grieving for the pretty, blond woman and her untimely death, or for her fortune, gained and lost? Perhaps both, and for a long time he treasured her memory, a Hope diamond in the iron vault of his mind, a casket stripped of the velvet cushioning of sentimentality.

Jerzy Kosinski, Katherina (Kiki) von Fraunhover (later to be his second wife), Carlos and Sylvia Fuentes, and my husband and I were on holiday in Venice, an unreal city, a lovely bubble, unsubstantial, amnesiac, a beachcomber's paradise. Bedecked in decay, it is drowning, slowly, in the polluted waters of its canals. On this visit I was to share my vision with friends native to different parts of the old world, (Carlos Fuentes and his wife, from Mexico City, Kiki von Fraunhover, a German, Kosinski, Polish), perhaps, through them at home in many places, I might solidify my view of Venice. When I explored churches, museums, palazzi, or crossed the expanse, great as a lake, of the Piazza San Marco with Carlos Fuentes, I had a cicerone who was, at once, an habitué and an erudite, curious foreigner. As for Jerzy Kosinski, he seemed to belong here, everywhere and nowhere.

On our last evening in Venice, we dined at the Hotel Cipriani, where Carlos and Sylvia were staying. Distanced by only meters of water from the main island, the hotel was an opposite world, with neither romance nor a past. A cheerful, luxurious, manicured resort, it had resisted the infection of art and decomposition situated nearby. The swimming pools, tennis courts and flower gardens were well tended, related to their own type in every country. In the sumptuous dining room, one rich international course followed the next, each dish covered with a shining silver dome. We ate and drank heartily, only Jerzy was abstemious, barely wetting his thin lips on his Champagne glass and nibbling on a sliver of toast with smoked salmon. He required scant ordinary nourishment, his electric vitality was fed by some other unknown source. That night, his discourse was sharp, abrasive, provocative, the ice-pellet words freezing even the brilliant conversation of Carlos Fuentes, who observed Kosinski with the attentiveness of the novelist always on the look out for material that might, someday, be utilized for his works.

On the dock, Kiki, Jerzy, my husband and I said good-bye to Carlos and Sylvia, promising to have a reunion soon, and we boarded the *vaporetto* for the brief return transit. Kosinski reclined among the pillows on the deck, but he did not relax, his body was an arrow ready to spring from a taut bow.

"The night has just begun for us," he said. "We usually hire a gondola at this hour to explore the back *callies*. Along the way we pick up prostitutes, here, sailors, there, and they join us aboard. We amuse ourselves in various ways."

I pictured this *Walpurgisnacht* orgy; Kiki, Amazonian and practical, bent to her master's will. Now we are approaching Venice, its domes and towers rising abruptly out of the water. In the flickering light on the *vaporetto*,

Kosinski's face had a compelling, eerie beauty, closed as a satanic mask worn by an eighteenth-century reveler at a ball in a Renaissance palazzo while it was still in full glory, before decay and threat of submersion. The evening at the Cipriani dwindled and vanished, consumed in a moment of timelessness against which the material is defenseless.

When we disembarked, Jerzy and Kiki moved off in one direction; we, in another. For no apparent reason, I looked back just as Kosinski and his companion were disappearing through the door of their hotel. And the floating brothel, had it only been invented for our benefit, another tale to shock the bourgeoisie? I experience an irrational disappointment, and, unexpectedly, a different scene out of my childhood returned to me. I was dining with my family at a French seaside resort, when my father announced that the Prince of Wales was sitting at the next table. Yet all I saw was an ordinary young man in golfing costume—no crown, no ermine bordered velvet robe, no scepter. Long later, on a street in Venice, in my mind's eye, I followed Kosinski through the lobby, into the lift, down the corridor to his hotel room, along a route identical to the one I would be taking shortly.

Through the years, it seemed to me that Kosinski's oral sagas were altering, the gypsy being replaced by the Jewish survivor of the Holocaust. But in my view, he remained a loner, affiliated with no group, without any shared history, descended from his own book *The Painted Bird*, unindebted to what is generally called factual.

Now, he often acted as chairman, fund raiser and orator for charitable events. He was effective as president of the American P.E.N. and on behalf of Amnesty International, and many a political prisoner might thank him for freedom. Introducing eastern European literature in the United States became a mission and just as once a dedicated socialist evoked the name of Karl Marx, Kosinski called upon Bruno Schulz, the late author, victim of the Nazis. One evening, from my place in an auditorium, I observed Kosinski on the podium, behind a microphone, delivering a money-raising speech for liberated Czechoslovakia. His voice was rasping, weaker, the words less staccato, but he appeared as stylish as ever. Yet like a ghost over his shoulder I saw a different figure: a Warsaw schoolboy, wearing an old-fashioned cap and an adult's overcoat, several sizes too large for him, from a pre-Holocaust photograph caught by the camera of Roman Vishnyac. Images of the ghetto population still unaware of its approaching fate, they break our hearts, and from our safe niche in place and time, we want to scream to warn those innocents arrested in suspended motion. The vision of the schoolboy faded and the renowned author stood alone on the stage.

I read in *The New York Times* the account of Jerzy Kosinski's macabre suicide. He was found dead, lying in his bathtub, his head bound inside a plastic shopping bag, his chosen implement for suffocation. I visualized his dark face showing through the transparent material, and it brought to mind the creations of the artist, Christo; the bridges of the river Seine wrapped in plastic shrouds, while the portentous stone gargoyles on the cathedral of Notre-Dame survey the scene, mutely. It was a shock to learn, later, that this way of taking one's life was not a final demonic gesture on the part of Jerzy Kosinski, but the method recommended by the Hemlock Society. What cause had triggered his death? I remembered being told by a survivor that the burden of Holocaust memories never grows lighter and may, at any moment, become too heavy to endure. That arrogant presence who trod the ground so lightly, was he the product of his own tricks and my fancy? Did I, as a Jew, wish to invest one of my own kind with supernatural invincibility? During all those years had I overlooked a human being? In any case, I am certain that Jerzy Kosinski would have scorned compassion.

I hasten to reread *The Painted Bird*.

Chapter Fifteen

PRIX DE ROME—CIRCA 1920

"The mural painter is a dodo bird,"* Thomas Winthrop told me as I sat enthroned on a gilded Renaissance chair in his lofty studio. But he seemed a caged lion, with his long torso, comparatively short legs and the padded sound of his tread. He wore espadrilles and a khaki paint-spattered smock, an old-fashioned artisan in the era of Abstract Expressionism. For it was the 1950s.

We had met recently and though, now, as his penetrating glance moved from me to his easel and back again—he was the maker—we eyed one another with reciprocal interest, as subject to subject, divided, in age, by a generation, as well as by our different backgrounds. I was impatient to trespass behind the easel, but he would not permit me to see the portrait unfinished; while my likeness of him, painted in my mind's eye, was ongoing, fluctuating, uncontained by the boundaries of the four sides of a rectangle.

*A large bird that formerly lived in Mauritius, but has long been extinct. (*Oxford American Dictionary*)

Thomas Winthrop was an indigenous American, a Mayflower descendant whose ancestors had settled in Wisconsin. "Plowmen," he described them but, to me, they were the nation's aristocrats.

My friend, Philip Rahv, co-founder of the *Partisan Review*, editor and critic, used to say in his heavy Russian-Yiddish accent, "Tom is a Fourth of July American."

And so he was. But, just as in a World War I photograph, a soldier in combat uniform, girded with guns, looks out from beneath his helmet with the smiling, innocent face of a boy, despite his surroundings—the Italianate furniture, the canvases stacked along the walls, and the aroma, an amalgam of paint, turpentine and new wood shavings, common to artists' studios the world over—Thomas Winthrop, his rugged height, rosy cheeks, snub nose with wide nostrils and his cleft chin, fulfilled my romantic portrait of a pioneer. He disliked his profile, saying, "When I was a boy, my mother used to clamp my nostrils with a clothespin, trying to give me an aristocratic, aquiline nose like my father's."

But in his small, deep-set eyes, I thought I detected the gaze, keen, stern and direct, of the small-town judge, his father.

When Tom put down his brushes and palette, I would wander around the studio examining his work. There was, usually, a long strip of paper tacked to a wall, a charcoal mock-up for a mural. I lingered longest over the oils—female nudes (sensual but economical in line, leaving room for the stirrings of the imagination), they had generous hips and, sometimes, swollen bellies, yet Thomas

Winthrop had never wanted children. There were, also, many versions of women's heads with Medusa locks, winged angels of destruction, and centaurs. From where did these fancies spring? Somehow I connected them to those footsteps on bare boards, the wild forest animal in a space too narrow for his leashed, unselfconscious strength.

Watching me, Thomas Winthrop said, "I am a 'Sunday painter.'"

Bit by bit I learned about his debut as an artist. In his teens he had volunteered in the First World War and, at the front as a private in the infantry, he had been severely wounded. Eventually, he had been shipped back to the United States for rehabilitation, where in an army hospital, as therapy, he had been given paints and brushes. I imagined his intoxication at this encounter—swift, unexpected yet mysteriously familiar—as love at first sight. After his release, he had begged his father for a year's trial as a painter in New York City, although it had always been assumed that he was going to follow his parent in the law.

"I lived in a basement room in the Bowery and visited the Chinese laundry to have my one good shirt washed and ironed. Although I knew few people, I was more exhilarated than lonely."

In his telling there was neither self-pity nor senti-mentality. His voice was soft, controlled, an echo of the muffled sound of his footfalls.

"I painted long hours," he continued, "and visited museums. At home, in Wisconsin, we had plenty of books; volumes of history, the classics and, of course, my father's law tomes. But I had never seen a painting, not even a reproduction. Like a man starving, I feasted on

everything—especially the Titians at the Metropolitan—
always feeling guilty that I wasn't following my father's
lead."

I pictured him wallowing in the sensuous pleasures
of art, like a young Puritan in the arms of a worldly,
voluptuous Mediterranean beauty.

"I never doubted that this way of living would be
over when the year was up."

But it was to be otherwise. Competitions in the
arts—hard work and talent notwithstanding—like winning
lottery tickets, depend, in large part, on chance. Lacking
credentials, contacts and formal training, Thomas Winthrop
applied for a Prix de Rome, and it was granted. To the end
of his days, he would light up at the prospect of a contest:
a Franklin Roosevelt or John Kennedy memorial, a plan for
the Audubon Society or for a veteran's cemetery in Great
Britain. Although he was usually a loser, his early experience had impressed itself upon his feelings and he would
enter the fray, optimistic and energetic as a youth. And, as
long as he lived, he would travel back to Rome, the city of
inspiration. When his term at the American Academy was
over, there remained the problem of earning a living, and
Thomas Winthrop chose mural painting, much in demand
at that time. His specialized métier had been decided.

With the arrival of the 1950s, Le Corbusier had
delivered his famous dictum, "a house is a machine for
living," calling for the decline of wall paintings, along with
other non-functional ornamentation. Oddly, Thomas Winthrop was attracted to this innovative simplicity. And, just as
a dedicated surgeon might observe the skilled knife cutting
into his own body, the painter watched, objectively, his

profession being incised by the new order. He was reduced to producing murals with no relation to the spaces they occupied and he grumbled that he was no longer consulted in the original concept. Only after a building had been erected, was he asked to affix a prescribed picture: blind-folded Justice with her scales, or George Washington crossing the Delaware, for the walls of anachronistic, neo-classical banks, post offices and courthouses. It was too late to change his course. He and Edna, his wife, did talk sometimes about moving to a tropical island where living would be cheap and he could paint as he pleased without worrying about money. But Tom was no bohemian and the genes of his industrious ancestors must have rebelled at the thought of becoming an "ivory tower" artist. I felt that, despite the frustrations, he enjoyed the physical activity of his profession. Watching him at the site of his work, atop a tall ladder, surrounded by scaffolding, his smock dusted in mortar, with his rugged frame and the tools of his trade, he looked a proper master-builder; only later did I realize that he was a Gulliver shackled by the pygmy tyranny of fashion.

"Postage stamps," he called these murals.

But unsatisfactory as they were, they helped to make possible his life style. For Tom, despite his Puritan con-science—possibly ignited by it—was a sybarite who loved the textures of rich fabrics, the luxury of spacious rooms and the elegance of beautiful women in evening dress. He and Edna gave gala parties in the Italianate studio. At night, the frayed spots on the brown velvet furniture and walls, exposed by the tactless light of day, were invisible; the gold claw-footed chair became a seat for a Doge and the mute pipes of a broken organ, rising three stories to the ceiling, were the columns of a Venetian palace. On one occasion, a string orchestra had been hired to play from the overhanging balcony. Tom was especially proud of the baronial fireplace, which he had built himself, stone by stone. In tuxedo, his black bow tie beneath his cleft chin, his face scrubbed and ruddy, he was impeccable. It was said that Thomas Winthrop looked like Dwight Eisenhower, but as I watched him circulating among his guests, it occurred to me that it was not the President he resembled, whose image had diminished like the mercury in a thermometer brought inside from the sun, but rather the World War II general (in mufti), a vigorous American presence profiled against the weary Old World.

The vehemence of Tom's outspoken opinions, however, was, at times, out of line. An autodidact, he was able to argue cogently on such topics as history, philosophy, politics, architecture, military tactics, and I knew that he even wrote poetry in secret. Although the people who attended the Winthrop's soirées were as various as his interests, in an age of specialization, the broad spectrum of this Renaissance man was regarded with suspicion, and Tom's impatient anger, released by wine, could be wounding. Edna attempted to avert fights; at her husband's side, loyal and admiring, she was like a tug nudging a large liner into its allotted berth. Avoiding controversy was especially necessary when an important architect was present, someone who might be influential in securing for Tom the type of work he desired.

Lincoln Center has been standing for so many years that it is difficult to remember that once it existed only as tentative plans on the drawing boards of architects attending the gatherings at the Winthrops' home, and the space waited, holding for all of us the expectations of the not yet executed. Tom, like a child before a bake shop window, regarded the chosen area with longing. Was he visualizing the Baths of Caricalla on Broadway, or the silhouette of a new world compound? He did not live long enough to see its realization—a compromise devised by a committee of well-known architects. In the windows of the Opera House, the paintings of Chagall hang extraneous to the general design; they, like the posters on the plaza outside that advertise the singers, proclaim with pride the painter's famous name.

One evening, long after Thomas Winthrop's death, I attended a symphony concert at Lincoln Center. The auditorium had been gutted again and again to improve its acoustics; until now it bore no likeness to the original but resembled the interior of a giant cigar box with wavy wooden protuberances, but when the music began, my surroundings blurred and melted like the vision of someone under the influence of the seed of the poppy. After the intermission, the orchestra played Mozart's *Jupiter Symphony*. I was invaded, all at once, by a strong smell—an amalgam of paint, turpentine and new wood shavings. Were they still working on the hall, and while a performance was going on? In a whisper, I asked my companon if she, too, had noticed the odor. She shook her head, no. But the smell continued to tease my nostrils, evaporating only with the finale of the Mozart symphony. I thought no more about it until, on my way home, I passed the apartment building where the Winthrops used to live. The number on the door meant no more to me, now, than an item crossed out in my address book. In front of the façade, just as a conjurer produces a string of knotted scarves from an empty hat, the chain of causes that had invoked the aroma in the concert hall was revealed to me. I recalled that Thomas Winthrop, during the many hours I had sat for him, had played the *Jupiter Symphony* on his phonograph, and so long afterwards, in a Witches Night of the senses, an impish whiff had invaded my ear as I listened to the music. The olfactory and the auditory were confounded, and the past had penetrated the thin membrane of the present. Standing on the street before Thomas Winthrop's door, I saw the studio emerge, intact, with all the magic of Venice rising from the sea.

Thomas Winthrop's last commission was for the National Cathedral under construction in Washington, D.C. He was enthusiastic, but I asked myself how a declared agnostic who had erupted from the dutiful pieties of his upbringing would approach this task, and I was surprised that the central figure of Christ proved to be so moving. Just as a centaur is part man, part animal, this version of Jesus appeared to be one with the throne on which he was placed; the human and the inorganic merged in a vision of mystical order and strength, so far from the accustomed mild, saintly image, that I worried lest the work be rejected. What had goaded Thomas Winthrop's imagination into producing this unorthodox symbol imbued, nonetheless, with love and reverence? Just as the recall of the quotidian from our childhood may acquire in time the radiance of a nimbus, it is my belief that Thomas Winthrop, having abandoned the traditions of his boyhood, as an aging man, living far off among different people, still treasured the example of his father. The portrayal derived subconsciously from his memory of a small-town judge's chair—crude, Gothic, upright—and the man who had sat upon it.

As the panels were to be mosaic, Thomas Winthrop and his wife left for Italy, where he could still find artisans skilled in that medium. I knew his joy at returning to Rome, as invigorating to him as is the air on the summit to a mountain climber. Back home, he praised those who had worked for him, saying, "We were like one family."

I pictured him with the young men who handled, expertly, the bits and pieces of stone, taking pleasure in their craft without thought of renown; and Tom, joining them, his blunt artist's fingers, like a Roman emperor's sifting emeralds, sapphires and rubies. And, just as someone feeling the approach of death prays for time to know a grandson, grown, a granddaughter, married, Thomas Winthrop, when he realized that he was mortally ill, wished to live long enough to return once again to Rome. But he never did see it again.

I made a pilgrimage to Washington to view the mosaic in place. The cathedral, in the way of its genre, was more city than single building. Unfinished, it would involve generations of artists and builders to complete its heterogeneous growth. Among the religious statues, paintings, the cluttered niches and transepts branching from the enormity of the central nave, in the demi-light, I had difficulty in locating Tom's mosaic. I found it high up, beneath the valuted ceiling, in a distant corner where it appeared smaller than I had remembered, and the singular figure of Jesus looked hardly different from the rest.

★ ★ ★

I saw Rome for the first time only after Thomas Winthrop's death. I had thought to experience the city through his eyes, but the sight of its time-layered beauty caused me to forget my yesterdays.

Before I left, in tribute to my friend, I climbed the Janiculum to the American Academy, a Mediterranean villa set in a lush park. But there was something rank about the profusion of tropical flowers, shrubs and parched palm trees that reminded me of a Garden of Eden in which the Fall is already foretold. I stood on the edge of the hill overlooking the view of Rome dominated by the beehive dome of St. Peter's and the mortuary white mass of the Victor Emanuel monument, an all-too-solid reminder of the dead dictator's fist. In the Forum, among the stones and toppled pedestals, the shades of the Caesars lurked, while across the expanse of sky, cloud sculptures floated, like the playful sea gods of Bernini's fountains set in motion. From some place out of the depths of the city, I heard the bucolic crowing of a rooster. Nothing is ever altogether lost.

Chapter Sixteen

THE HERALDIST

> What are little girls made of?
> Sugar and spice and everything nice,
> What are little boys made of?
> Snips and snails and puppy dog tails—
> —fragment from a nineteenth-
> century nursery rhyme

The photograph, blown up over life size, reigned on a wall of the foyer of Lillian Hellman's apartment on Park Avenue. A monumental presence, it confronted the visitor upon entering. Long ago, a camera caught the image of a majestic black woman, dressed in a prim, starched Victorian shirt-waist, her gray hair pulled severely back; stiffly erect, she towers above a small girl child, dolled up for the sitting in party frock and white-buttoned shoes, who hugs the nanny's long, dark skirt like lichen to the trunk of a tree. Neither the passage of the years, nor the fame and sophistication of Lillian Hellman, playwright and memoirist, has dimmed the mythology of this pair: the regal servant and the "sassy" white babe. Yet the facts tell us that Sophronia was employed only briefly as wet-nurse by the Hellman family, and Lillian, as she grew up, was obliged to seek out her private oracle at the home of strangers, where two boys in her charge were oblivious to the homespun sage in their midst. An exaggerated shadow, the photograph followed Lillian in her various dwellings. And just as a woman noted for contemporary chic likes to cloak herself in threadbare costumes from her attic, Lillian Hellman masquerades in the feather boa fantasies of the South.

Yet, in the main, her home had been New York City and she was the only child of German-Jewish parents whose family had emigrated to Louisiana and Alabama in the mid-nineteenth century. It is true that in her youth Lillian spent several months of the year with her father's spinster sisters who ran a shabby boarding house in New Orleans. Their antiquated standards and restraints sometimes clashed with the strong will of their hoyden niece, serving to enhance their sentimental value in the memories of the writer; for Lillian, a fight would always be more desirable than peace; enemies, more stimulating than friends.

On an evening in late May, 1984, my husband and I were unaware that it was to be our last meeting with Lillian Hellman. A few weeks later she died at Martha's Vineyard, ending a friendship spanning more than twenty years. After paying my respects to the photograph of Sophronia in the hall, I entered the living room where our hostess greeted us from a red velvet Victorian settee. Too ill to rise, she was crippled, virtually blind and suffered from emphysema, which did nothing to slow down the compulsiveness of her chain-smoking. That night, she was wearing a scarlet gown, cut low enough to reveal the subcutaneous mound of a pace-maker, like a new, miniature grave about her heart. She had just been to the hairdresser and her long, swinging bob, in the fashion of a 1940 debutante, was freshly waved and dyed a brilliant golden blond. Her mouth, with its slash of lipstick the hue of dried blood, was san open wound, and her high-bridged nose jutted like the prow of a schooner from a face lined as an explorer's map. But the traces of Lillian Hellman's years of adventure were to find more permanent recordings in the pages of her memoirs. It is my belief, however, that she would gladly have traded all her success in exchange for the pretty kitten features of a belle, a white pillared mansion and an indigenous Southern lineage.

When we moved to the dining table, two nurses appeared, silently, to assist her. Dinner was served by a black woman, the last of a line that attempted to recover Sophronia. Our hostess, frequently wracked by that shattering cough, nevertheless led the conversation, her wit as sharp as ever, if even more acid; her vocabulary tangy as a stevedore's, her laughter, robust like the cough, threatened the precarious assemblage of her body. I marvelled at her fight and resented the attempts of a nurse to push food into her resisting mouth. But Lillian waved the fork away, absently, as though she were merely swatting an annoying housefly.

"Last winter in California was great," she told us. She had been the guest of one of those young male friends who attended her with the gallantry of suitors. "But I couldn't work on my book. I have very bad writer's block!"

So near to death and still able to complain about writer's block!

"Tell me about the book—" I began, but was halted abruptly. I had intercepted the glance of the black serving maid. Hatred, mute and murderous, was beamed at her employer. Was Lillian a difficult mistress, cantankerous, overexacting, or were those the poisonous rays of New

York City's racial hatreds? This, then, was the conclusion of the Southern fable. For an instant, I was relieved that Lillian was unable to see.

Returned to the living room, I dodged the burning cigarette, removing it from Lillian's wavering hand and crushing it into the littered ashtray. But she had already inserted another into the gash of her lips, requesting my husband to light it for her. On a drum table beside me a Tiffany lampshade showered its stained-glass glow upon two photographic portraits in embossed silver frames: Lillian's mother and Dashiell Hammett, her lover, off and on, for about thirty years. The mother appears young in the picture, but her mild face is rendered insignificant by the elaborateness of her coiffure, and her body is disguised and deformed by bustle and stays; her bosom, capacious as an overstuffed cushion swathed in lace and satin. In the living room, no likeness of Lillian's father is to be found, although I had learned from the memoirs that she had been closer to him than to her mother. But as a salesman never quite able to provide adequately for his wife and daughter, he was excluded from the pictorial pantheon. One of Lillian's passionate contradictions would always be her love-hate relationship to money. Her most acclaimed plays have dramatized the maternal clan, their greed, ugly materialism and their incessant squabbling about fortunes made and lost. Although she relates that at family gatherings she stood apart, disgusted, and despite the fact of her own considerable earnings and her luxurious life-style, wealth continued to attract her like an unconsummated affair.

Nowhere in her dramas is there mention of Jews. And, just as a set of Louis XV chairs is overlaid by paint, covered in tapestry, hiding the basic material beneath, these creations also conceal, denying in recall, the fine wood grain of geniune family history.

Willy, an uncle, the husband of her mother's sister, is a major gargoyle in her memoirs, he upholds the walls of their shaky genealogy. Sufficiently seductive to merit a chapter to himself in the pages of *Pentimento*, he is traditionally equipped with an invalid, drug-addicted wife, a retarded son and mysterious Mafia-like business connections. The adolescent Lillian fell in love with him, almost— saved from actual incest at the last moment through some clever "spunky," if nebulous, action of her own. The "Willy" episode would prove to be a prototype for her future amorous ambiguities: romance and outrage mingling, as they would, throughout her life.

One might wonder at the proximity of these two silver-framed photographs bathed in the prismatic cathedral light of the Tiffany lamp. In contrast to the mother, the image of Dashiell Hammett is lean, keenly dark-eyed. An unregenerate Communist, he had been a Pinkerton detective, tough soldier and the author of widely popular cool, street-smart murder mysteries; and he was to play, throughout his affair with Lillian, the role of indispensable tutor. Their love was expressed, Hemingway style, waged through fierce physical combat, drunken scenes, infidelities on both sides and hard-won reconciliations. Housewife-mother and apache-lover, I doubt they ever met, but they were linked through their photographs, forming two sections of Lillian Hellman's contradictory self-constructed emotional coat-of-arms, emblematic of proud old money and stubborn pro-Stalinist communism. A third part was occupied by

Sophronia, African queen-nurse. Thus armored, Lillian, female knight, ventured forth, aggressive, yet questioning, forever in need of a mentor. ". . . Dash, show me how. . . . Tell me what is right." "Sophronia, answer me. You know truth," the adult's plea merging with the treble voice of the girl-child from a past gilded by wishful visions of Southern aristocratic affluence. And yet, Lillian remained a staunch apologist for Stalinism long after her associates had fallen away.

"Bah," my friend, Philp Rahv, bitter anti-Stalinist, disillusioned Trotskyite, used to say "Wid Lillian it iss all romance. She was never political, not truly a Red. She tink she and Dash are Tristan and Isolde. Everyting iss in de imagination. She iss a romantic, tru and tru, forever revising de facts!" But his rough voice issuing from his bear-like person did not sound unkind. Rather, it reminded me of a shrewd country doctor who has just diagnosed an illness, chronic but not fatal.

His words returned to me on an evening in which Lillian and I were alone in her town house in the East eighties, near Madison Avenue. One of a row of similar façades, it was part of a residential block for the privileged. Now, when I pass that particular door, I seem to see her name permanently carved into the lintel. Perhaps it was in this home that she fancied she had recaptured an echo of her mother's early days of Southern cordiality while the Park Avenue apartment represented in her scornful view the displeasing conventions of New York City "nouveau riche." In her town house Lillian gave many parties. She was a good hostess who liked to prepare favorite Cajun dishes herself. A celebrity, she enjoyed collecting other celebrities who were attracted by her hospitality, her cleverness and humor. In the tasseled, portiered rooms one could find a cross-section of intellectuals, artists, musicians, politicians, tycoons and, of course, theatre people. Despite her foremost position as playwright, there was always a note of disparagement when she spoke about Broadway.

"I enter the theatre, young," she would say, "full of hope; but when I leave, I am hopeless and greatly aged!"

For Hollywood, even before the McCarthy era, she displayed nothing but the strongest of her famous venom. That evening we sat side by side on the velvet sofa, located then in the town house. We laughed a great deal and, as usual with Lillian, I experienced a sense of camaraderie that I mistrusted as soon as we were apart. Suddenly, she moved closer, her face so near that her features appeared alarmingly enlarged, distorted into a mask of rage.

"Do you realize that your husband is a malefactor?" she asked.

Stunned by the unexpected assault, I barely managed to inquire the reason.

But Lillian was launched. "He publishes Solzhenitsyn," she snapped.

"Surely, he has the right." I began.

"What right?" she interrupted. "What is right? Roger is wrong. Solzhenitsyn is evil, he is the Devil. Furthermore, if you knew what I know about American prisons, you would be a Stalinist, too!"

I felt bewildered, like Alice in the wake of the senseless tantrums of the Duchess in Wonderland. Were Roger and I about to join the swelling ranks of Lillian's enemies?

"It iss all Tristan and Isolde." I heard the voice of Philip Rahv again. And Fidelio, too, I thought. With Dashiell Hammett, Lillian Hellman had quaffed the magic love potion, in this instance spiked with communist zeal; later, like Leonora in Beethoven's opera, she had fought to free her beloved from jail. She supported Hammett in financial ruin until his death, and the opera curtain would fall only with her own end.

She must have forgotten Roger's crime, I mused, as we three sat in amity at that last meeting. Or, perhaps, it was another of those violent contradictions that Lillian thrived on, because I noted that she addressed him in that flirtatious manner she reserved for successful, masterful males; a Southern lady's subservience sugar-coating her own peppery aggressiveness.

In my mind's eye, I passed in review the antitheses in the scenario of Hellman's life: the willful tomboy, the well brought-up little miss, the daring reporter (Spanish Civil War and Russian front), the gracious salonkeeper, the suburban farmer, the veteran playwright nervously vomiting in the ladies' room on opening night, the good chum, the dangerous foe, the self-proclaimed heroine, the hero-worshipper, the witness, dramatically waving her right to take the Fifth Amendment while testifying before the House Un-American Activities Committee and wearing an expensive French import purchased especially for the occasion!

With that pseudo-frank modesty that was actually swagger, I had often heard her disclaim, "I was never brave, you know. I would just ask myself what Hammett would want me to do, and then I did it. I am really a natural coward."

When Roger and I moved to leave, the silent nurses reappeared, as though radar-directed, to lead Lillian to her bedroom rigged like a medical station on some other planet: bells, light signals, wires, tubes and tanks at readiness. The antique double bed, from her mother's Alabama home, had been pushed aside for the nurse's use. Lillian occupied a hospital cot with mechanical devices that could bring her no ease.

"Stay awhile," she begged, "I'll be ready in a minute."

We found her propped in her hospital bed, in a coquettish short pink nightgown that revealed her thin, brittle legs knotted by varicose veins. And just as butterflies may survive the dead season at summer's end, two pink bows quivered on lace straps that kept slipping down from her skeletal shoulders. Like someone who averts her eyes from an accident, I turned away, more in horror than in pity from this moribund frivolity. Her conversation, however, continued animated, witty and wicked, interrupted by the blast of that shattering cough. The nurse remained in the room with us, sitting mutely on the edge of the great heirloom bed, her silence expressing disapproval rather than shyness. When at last we said good-bye to her, Lillian clung to our hands.

"Don't forget that you are coming to visit me at the Vineyard," she reminded us.

The heraldist is dead. The pieces of her escutcheon have been scattered as illustrations for her books. Known for her audacity, sexual liberation, an elder feminist with a combative stance, a cantankerous partisan, she was, also, a woman of paradox who yearned to claim as her own the background of an upper-class, genteel Southern Victorian childhood. As I was writing this memoir, a fragment of a long-forgotten nursery rhyme (quaint when I first heard it, archaic now), presented itself as inscription for Lillian Hellman's blazon. The heraldist's dreams are romantic, incongruous, unrealized.

Chapter Seventeen

A VOICE FROM THE FIRST GENERATION

Bernard Malamud and his wife, Ann, dined with us on an evening in 1986, when, in his words, "winter was on its last legs." On the surface, the gathering resembled many others we had shared, dating back thirty years. During that time there were, also, readings by Malamud of his work in progress at his home on West 70th Street, and at an assortment of parties where we met—I can name a whole population of fellow guests—but at this dinner, try as I may, I remember only Bern.

I see his slow, yet unhesitating entrance into our living room. He had been in poor health, but, in his peaceable fashion, Bern was a fighter and neither illness nor his age (seventy-one) had managed to make inroads into his essential, idiosyncratic self. He appeared smaller than before, but the observant intelligence of his brown eyes, behind spectacles, was as unflinching as ever. They spoke for him, as well as his speech (which was slower, now, too). Talking to Bernard Malamud could never be a disappointing experience; at a dining room table or seated, companionably, on a sofa, he has taught me more than any professor on a dais.

I am able to record only a few phrases, out of context, but I hoard them. They are both larger and lesser than when they were uttered. "What do years matter as long as they are not wasted? Each one that comes makes better the bargain," or, "the human being is imperfect . . . the ideal is not . . ." Malamud, the consummate writer of fiction, part teacher, part scholar, was always a striver whose seriousness was tempered by his special brand of wry humor. In one of his most powerful fable-type stories, *The Last Mohican*, the anti-hero, Fidelman, a failed artist, and his ghostly counterpart, the peddler, duel in words, at once comic and sinister.

We often talked about our favorite authors—especially the nineteenth-century Russians, Marcel Proust and Virginia Woolf. On this evening, sitting next to one another at the table, we seemed to pick up our conversation where we had left off the time before. We were actors taking part in a long run, and I had no intimation that the play was about to close.

After dinner, Malamud rose from his chair, early, "I must go home now," he said, "tomorrow there will be a long morning of work on my novel."

I followed his cautious step down the stairs. And, with Ann beside him, I saw him disappear into the street.

At about noon the next day, Bernard Malamud died at his worktable, while fulfilling his resolutions—his last hours, unwasted.

Despite my awareness of his precarious health, the shock was great—and the loss. Many other memories of him have been expunged by the sad, inadvertent drama of that good-bye. But the night of March, 1986, is with me. Seated at my right, there is Bern with his cup of tea, as usual. The years have brought a measure of consolation to the recall of the last meeting, at the very end of Bernard Malamud's life I was privileged to find in him no diminution. His wisdom, his humor, his pride, as well as his humility were intact.

Now, when I reread his wonderful stories, I discover him again, the frail, strong man; the secular Jew with his firm code of ethics; his belief in reason—product of the enlightenment, the American Diaspora, master of paradox, who, in his writing, often glanced back ruefully and with some regret, to a mystical past he could no longer espouse.

Bern, I know you hated to be classified as a "Jewish writer." I agree that all categories (black, woman, Jew) are reductive. Yet, if I may venture a paradox, myself, I believe that your spirit, as well as the engaging cadence of your prose, are, indeed, quintessential first-generation Jewish. And I am grateful. You have given testimony to best of kind—through your writings and in your person.

During my childhood I was unaware of the existence of Ellis Island. And I have never learned the name of the port of entry used by my ancestors, German Jews, who arrived in this country with the wave of immigration of 1848. Yet, today, Ellis Island is a favorite tourist site for the ethnically conscious citizens of New York City who come in flocks to inspect its bare halls in memory of the thousands who passed through at the turn of the century, on their way to becoming Americans. But when I was growing up, in the days before the Holocaust, we discarded our history as Jews, and just as people in good health avoid contact with tuberculosis, still insecure, we feared contagion from the new Jewish arrivals from the ghettos of Eastern Europe, uninoculated with the remedies (now outmoded) from the "melting pot."

In the late nineteenth century, the young Alfred Stieglitz, himself a wealthy German Jew, photographed *Steerage* (in my view, a picture more sentimental than moving) from the vantage of first class aboard an ocean liner. In the crowd on the lower, uncovered deck, one might recognize the face of the Russian, Morris Bober, out of *The Assistant*, a novel by Bernard Malamud. The son of an immigrant, the author used his father as model; a memorial more vital than the preserved stones and halls of Ellis Island.

The action of *The Assistant* is confined to a block in a low-income section of the Bronx, one rung up the ladder from the East Side ghetto. Here, among poor Jews and Gentiles, Morris Bober, a grocer, ekes his meager living. The reader becomes familiar with the cans of soup, cold meats and three penny rolls on the shelves; with Morris, one waits for the all-to-infrequent ring of the cash register and one watches Bober's awkward descent from the cramped family apartment upstairs above the shop, at dawn, his weary return at night. Though physically weak, the grocer is fortified by his unswerving adherence to the Law. Just as the roof and four walls of a house in his own country are protection for most human beings, for the ghetto Jew of the Diaspora, the *Torah* and the *Talmud* constitute an internal home, transportable from one alien land to another. When we meet Morris, he has already evolved from the strict ritual of orthodoxy, but his allegiance to Jewish law remains intact. In an expressive amalgam of Yiddish-American, Morris talks to Frank Alpine, his Italian-Gentile assistant, a reformed tramp and petty criminal.

"This is not important to me if I taste pig or I don't. To some Jews, this is important, but not to me. Nobody will tell me that I am not Jewish because I put in my mouth, once in a while when my tongue is dry, a piece of ham. But they will tell me and I will believe them if I forget the Law. This means do what is right, to be honest, to be good. This means to other people. Our life is hard enough. Why should we hurt someone else? For everybody should be the best, not only for you and me. We ain't animals. This is why we need the Law. This is what a Jew believes."

When Frank answers that other religions have these ideas, but that "Jews suffer so damn much, it seems they like to suffer—" Morris says,

"If you live you suffer. Some people suffer more, but not because they want. But I think if a Jew don't suffer for the Law, he will suffer for nothing."

Despite the sadness, a continuous river flowing through the book, there is, also, a current of vigorous, ironic humor, indigenous to many Jewish fiction writers, Malamud, especially. Speaking of his hard lot, the grocer has the detachment to query, "How complicated could impossible get?"

Bernard Malamud, a consummate storyteller, is, as well, a wise, compassionate psychologist, who deals with sexual passions, family loyalties and quarrels, envy, hope, fears, ambitions, he knows about sleazy deals and crimes and he finds lofty generosity where it is least expected. Although Morris Bober is an anti-hero, gentle, seedy, stumbling, his inner dignity, his courageous patience, his patient courage raise him up to warrior without weapons. The characters in the book are various, although Malamud uses a minimum of description; in spare, telling strokes, through dialogue and behavior, his people come alive with all their blemishes and beauty, psychic as well as physical.

Following the grocer's death, the assistant, who has been working for almost no pay to atone for an earlier hold-up of the store, steps symbolically into his employer's shabby shoes in an attempt to resuscitate the failing business, and Frank Alpine continues to be stubbornly in love with the grocer's daughter, in spite of the gulf of race and culture. The relationship is left unresolved, intermarriage remains a question—a viable future for Jews?—or an ancient, unalterable transgression? Malamud offers no utopian solution: But the book concludes with a violent act of assimilation, in reverse: Frank Alpine, the Christian, has himself circumcised. "After Passover, he became a Jew." With this sentence, the story ends.

The world of the turn-of-the-century Jewish immigrant in New York has vanished, the first generation is going, too, but the voice of Bernard Malamud continues to resonate.

Chapter Eighteen

EPITAPH OF A MODEST NEW ENGLAND HOUSE

"You will recognize my house by the sign Petite Plaisance, and by the fields in front of it," said the writer, Marguerite Yourcenar.

Petite Plaisance, the name sounded, at once, regal and casual and combined with the vision of a sweep of acres. It conjured up in my mind's eye, a picture of one of those purportedly small chateaus, resembling the photographs that used to hang in the compartments of the French trains. It would be my first meeting with Madame Yourcenar and from her books it seemed fitting to find her in a dwelling only slightly less splendid than the palace of a king—a royal retreat like Josephine Bonaparte's Malmaison or the Petit Trianon of Marie-Antoinette—for her writings are aristocratic, self-assured, products of an old culture and scholarship, each book bearing the stamp of a rightful monarch of letters.

But Marguerite Yourcenar (the pen name is an acronym from the original, de Crayencour), born in Brussels of a Belgian mother and French father, no longer lived in Europe. She had been relocated for many years at Mount Desert Island, Maine. So pilgrimage there was thronged with the usual summer weekend travelers to New England. At take-off at Bar Harbor, the local, one-engine propeller plane spluttered and coughed as if to shatter its rickety sides. But, just as an ancient servitor resists retirement and relegation to a nursing home, faced with its inevitable end in the junk yard, the taxi plane rose haltingly off the ground. There was no *post chaise*, nor caparisoned horses to take us to Petite Plaisance.

Madame Yourcenar had reserved a room at the best inn at Northeast Harbor, close to where she lived. As I entered the lobby, I felt cool relief from the intense noonday heat outdoors but, at the same time, an amorphous psychic chill. The lobby was welcoming enough, a comfortable American turn-of-the-century period piece. The delectable smell of freshly baked bread drifted from the dining room, lingering after a hearty New England breakfast that was as much a part of the inn, I was to discover, as the repeated story of the great fire in 1889 that had destroyed the whole structure. But it had been rebuilt, a duplicate of the original: walls painted lemon-yellow, dormer windows, even the obsolete exterior fire escapes, climbing the façade, had been replaced. At the back of the reception room, tall windows opened to a splendid view of the marina, crowded with white sails as burgeoning as lilies. From the wooded hills surrounding the inlet, here and there, a roof, a wall, door or window—bits and pieces belonging to the spacious homes of the wealthy vacationers from Boston, Providence, Philadelphia and New York, peeked through the dense green. They seemed to proclaim: This forest belongs to us, our preserve; the ocean is our swimming hole, the marina a nautical playpen.

On the veranda of the hotel, hanging over a bluff open to the gracious scene, lounge chairs were aligned like Chinese dragons. Each one was preempted by an elderly woman in similar pastel summer attire, though the long white dressed, picture hats and parasols of Edith Wharton's heroines would have suited better. For the ladies on the porch, the swaying sails must have been melancholy reminders of former days when they, too, had boated and commandeered large households of servants and children of their own. Now, at the inn, they sat on the veranda, useless; gossiping, busy with their knitting and bridge games, waiting the arrival of another meal hour, punctual as the chimes of the grandfather's clock in the lobby.

Following Marguerite Yourcenar's directions, my husband and I walked along the street of her town in search of Petite Plaisance. We passed the usual village shops and the modest homes, each with its parsimonious allotment of front lawn. At the end of the road we came to a tall, fieldstone wall with an iron grill gate, the entrance to an estate. But the name outside was unknown. Beyond, there was only virgin woods. Puzzled, we retraced our steps, reading each sign with care. In front of a small shingle house, no different from its neighbors, with a stingy square of grass spread before it like a mat, we saw with disbelief, the name: Petite Plaisance. We had arrived.

Upon entering, the interior was so obscure that I was able to distinguish our hostess only in silhouette: a massive form moving with measured dignity to greet us. The voice was calm, mannish, the words strongly French accented. She seemed to fill the limited space to brimming, and like a classical structure rising above an overcrowded district, she dwarfed the clutter of furniture. Growing accustomed to the interior twilight, I was now able to discern the pillared cupboard, the claw-footed chairs and tables, gilt trimmed, the heavy, wintry burgundy red-tasseled curtains of a *bel époque*, urban, bourgeois decor. As in a dream, I groped for that other place that my imagination had created, more real than this solid setting in which I found myself. But just as someone who falls out of love is confounded when he sees, finally, the real object of his obsession, and relinquishes that other image, I was forced to forego the aristocratic retreat of my fancy and to accept this stuffy salon on the main street of a New England village.

Marguerite Yourcenar and my husband, her publisher, were discussing the publication of a forthcoming book on the Japanese writer, Mishima. I had leisure to examine her, and her appearance, unlike her setting was not at variance with my expectations. The creator of *Memoirs of Hadrian* looked more imperial Roman than French. Nearing eighty, she remained ageless, her ponderous body denoting power rather than excess. Her head was large, sculptural, the white hair brushed back from a spacious brow. Her features were generous, only the eyes, under heavy brows, were small, of undetermined color, as if the acute intelligence of their glance, like some strong acid, had burned away pigment, leaving only spark and depth.

A miniature gray poodle bounded into the room, interrupting the business discussion. I noted a new tone of tenderness in Marguerite Yourcenar's voice as she said: "This is Trier. He is the latest in a long line of pets. Soon, I will show you my dog cemetery in the garden."

A dog's cemetery! Hadrian's tomb would have been less surprising!

She continued talking about the book in progress. No detail—jacket design, type, the quality of paper—was overlooked. She had strong opinions on everything, her courteous suggestions had been thought through with meticulous care. And yet, there were manuscript pages scattered everywhere, on every inch of space. They seemed to flutter like wings and, at first glance, I feared that something would be lost. However, Yourcenar's serenity reassured me. Other authors might require more outward order, but the prose of Marguerite Yourcenar has the beauty of perfect control: This outward flurry of paper, any domestic disorderliness, could only be apparent.

We sat down to lunch at a small table next to the living room window facing the street, partially hidden by those wine red portieres. And I seemed to hear the sounds of the Paris of the Second Empire issuing from behind their stately folds, the clopping of horseshoes on cobblestones, the cries of street vendors, and the smell of sausage hanging outside a neighboring butcher shop. Most certainly, the meaty smell was not from our frugal meal. A bowl of shiny cranberries, resembling old-fashioned milliner's trim, was placed at the center of the table, flanked by salad greens, Greek olives and coarse, crusty peasant bread.

"I grow these berries myself," said Marguerite Yourcenar, handing the dish with pride.

I watched her as she ate. Here was no sated emperor, nor was she an ascetic. She tasted the cranberries thoughtfully, as though to extract their very essence.

Marguerite Yourcenar was sensual, sentient, a potentate who, having lived through a rich variety of sensory experience, had come to relish the ordinary fruits of the world with a connoisseur's pleasure born of past hedonism now tempered by the mellow autumnal wisdom of age. It was no accident that her remarkable "imaginary" memoir of the Emperor Hadrian was in the works for about thirty years. Often begun, often interrupted by travel, war, love, illness, but still there until the writer's voice merged with that other one, dusty with time, and the completed book seemed more an act of magicianly perpetuity than a contrived memoir. Here at a luncheon table in Maine sat Marguerite Yourcenar, the alchemist who had made this fusion, delecting in her homegrown cranberries, like the aging Emperor himself experimenting with his sophisticated senses. While, to my uneducated palate, the fruit tasted merely bitter.

After lunch, as she had promised, we looked at her garden, the site of the dog cemetery, at the back of the house. The forest crept around the sunny area, dark and unfathomable, causing the frail blooms to appear valiant and transitory. It would have been easy to miss the graves marked by flat paving stones if she had not pointed them out, while, Trier, the current companion, ran about insouciantly among the memorials to his predecessors.

My husband and I stayed until late, talking of many things, mainly about several books planned for the future.

"If time is given me," she added serenely.

Her conversation was detached, her ego required neither adulation nor boasting to sustain it. I told her that I had been reading *Archives du nord*, a memoir-biography that opens with a sketch of Flanders in the age of the caveman.

At the advent of the late Middle Ages, Madame Yourcenar is able to weave into her book the histories of members of her father's Flemish-French ancestry (landowners, petty nobility, bourgeoisie), with the somber earth-toned threads of an antique tapestry, here and there, effaced by age. By the nineteenth century, the memoir grows more detailed and personal, but the book concludes with the birth of the author.

She told us that she was considering a sequel to her diptych (the first volume, inversely, begins with her birth and travels back a generation) ". . . but I will stop when I am fifteen," she said. "No one should attempt to write about oneself beyond that age, one becomes self-conscious, the temptation to embellish is too strong—and, after all, is it so important?"

When we left, she accompanied us to the entrance. She had thrown a thin, white wool scarf over her head, protection against the cool Maine evening descending. Now she resembled a monument to the European immigrant. Yet she could not be regarded as an exile. French (the first woman to be admitted to their Academy), Belgian, New England townswoman, world traveler—she was all of these, and none. Her country lay behind her capacious forehead and its wealth in the rich and varied produce of her prose.

At the inn, it was dinner time. The aging widows and divorcées were descending the stairs, gingerly. Some were already sitting in the lounge waiting for the dining room doors to open. They had changed from their day costumes to drooping evening chiffons. And they wore, discreetly, jewels extracted from collections prudently stored in their bank vaults, glittering emblems to remind themselves and one another that they were emeritus, retired from a better life style, reduced in pleasure, perhaps, but not in status. Like a Greek chorus in flowered draperies, earrings, clips and necklaces, they lamented the passing of youth in falsely chirping voices. As we followed the crowd of fluttering, chatting dowagers into the dining room, I was thankful for that other existence in a saltbox house nearby. I could not help contrasting the old wax-work figures at the inn with that solitary, imperial presence. Was she writing at her desk, surrounded by a storm of manuscript pages? Perhaps she was just sitting in her armchair, musing, with Trier, the last of a succession of favorites, at her feet.

Marguerite Yourcenar has died. Like the Emperor Hadrian, she suffered from vascular disease and, like him, also, I am certain she watched the course of her own end with melancholy, scientific, philosophical interest, until, at last, she, too, was able to say to herself: "I am beginning to discern the profile of death." Surprisingly, she bequeathed Petite Plaisance to the town as a museum, and she is buried in the local cemetery. I do not believe that many pilgrims will visit her memorials in Mount Desert Island.

Let us look once more at this unassuming house, its obscure history and the obscure people connected with it. Early, perhaps in the eighteenth century, long ago in the annals of American settlers, a carpenter built its uncompli- cated frame and covered it with simple wood shingles that could weather harsh, salt wind. A glazier inserted window- panes (years later, smothered in deep red drapes, by a French author). Generations of housewives polished, swept, kneaded, scoured, mended and preserved the clearing against the encroachment of the forest where wild life roamed and died. Their village men were hunters, fishermen, and the lighthouse on the bluff welcomed the mariners when they returned to harbor. The small house was not visible at once, but a candle in the front parlor window at night summoned homeward.

I have chosen to close this memoir with a bow to Petite Plaisance: palace of a kind. There could be no better model than Marguerite Yourcenar's inspired serenade to the château of Chenonceaux.★

> A visit to old houses can lead to points of view we did not anticipate.

★*The Dark Brain of Piranesi and Other Essays. Ah Mon Beau Château* translated by Richard Howard in collaboration with the author. Farrar, Straus & Giroux.

Chapter Nineteen

THE LETTER WRITER

For quite some time I have lived in a high-rise on a block of private residences, brownstones that have been converted so that, like human beings, each displays individual characteristics. One has a bulging bay window that resembles a middle-aged pot belly; its neighbor's façade is heavily bearded in ivy; and the strawberry-pink mansion on the corner, uninhabited for generations, is as lifeless as an ugly princess under a spell in a fairy story. Across the street, a church and its red brick parish house occupy most of the block. Season in, season out, a homeless man with bare scabrous legs sits before the main portal. The sound of my coin falling into his paper cup is a tiny chime, and occasionally, I overhear a pedestrian murmuring a prayer to the white stone Madonna standing in the cramped church yard planted with roses and a single apple tree. I think of thousands of feet that have pounded these pavements and have disappeared, as mine will, too, some day.

Only now, when I recall him for the purpose of this memoir, do I realize that my good friend, Charles Jackson, used to live on this street. He had purchased his house from the proceeds of his autobiographical novel, *The Lost Weekend*, a "best seller" about an alcoholic. After he and his family had moved to Orford, New Hampshire, whenever he passed this area, he would point out his former home, with pride, saying, "that's the one." But since his death, about twenty years ago, this particular residence has been noteworthy, for me, only because in passing, I had glimpsed the prominent, fleshy nose of Richard Nixon in the parting of the lace curtains of the parlor window. I had forgotten that my friend, Charles Jackson, had stood before him on that very spot.

Even when we say, "I remember," the claim is often devoid of content, like an ungrammatical sentence without a subject. When I reminisce about "Charlie" with his youngest daughter, now an adult, although we are fond of one another, our memories are unshared. For her he is "papa," while the friend continues to elude me. But when I hear Schubert's *Trout* quintet rippling, melodious, carefree (a musical work introduced to me by Charles Jackson), I feel his presence resurrected from oblivion.

Now, years after Charles Jackson's death, I begin to understand the basis of our deep but ill-assorted companionship. Unlike passion, friendship has its reasons, and, perhaps, in uncovering these, I may atone for the disloyalty of my amnesia.

It may be only in hindsight that I believe that I "fell" into friendship "at first sight." It was at a writer's conference at Marlboro, Vermont, that I first saw Charles Jackson, and for me, he immediately became the focal point of the group seated in bucolic, bohemian informality in a field in front of a red barn. This scene may be inaccurate, also, engendered by the truthful lies of memory, but it cannot be erased. He was a small man, plump rather than stout, with smooth appetizing, polished skin that reminded me of the shells of chestnuts I used to collect in my childhood. He had a bald pate (although, at this time, he was in early middle age); his faintly Oriental brown eyes were, at once, mysterious, innocent and curious; his nose was pointed like a sandpiper's, made, I fancied, to ferret out odds and ends of gossip and human behavior, the raw material for his novels and stories; his mouth, beneath a neat black mustache was round and sensual. He wore a freshly ironed pink Brooks Brothers' shirt with a bow tie. His prim appearance contradicted what I knew of him: the drinking, homosexual encounters and attraction to "rough trade." Rather, he looked the warm family man he was also, and the small-town citizen of upstate Newark, New York, where he grew up and which in some sense, he never left. There was little in this portrait to draw me, and it is possible that, in reality, it did not do so on that hot July day, with its smell of baking hay and its aura of literature oddly trans-planted, like a White Russian emigré who drives a taxi in some alien city far from his native Petrograd.

I am able to remember only two others out of the group, and I am glad to have known them because, today, I am aware that they both belonged to endangered species. Ludwig Lewisohn, a famous author at that time, was an ardent Zionist as well as a scholar of classic German literature, a combination rare among later post-Holocaust writers. He had a massive, dignified head, a flowing mane of white hair, an air of eminence that reminded me of a bronze bust of Beethoven in the "music room" of my childhood home. He might have been found enthroned, in stately fashion, on a bench that would be marked, with a commemorative plaque of fame, like Goethe's sitz-platz, located in the formal park of a European spa I visited during summer travels with my family. Instead, memory has placed him squatting on the prickly unmowed grass in Marlboro, Vermont, with the rest of us.

The other person is Vincent Sheehan, member of a breed wiped out by television's coverage of the news, in which technological immediacy has supplanted the roamings, courageous and romantic of the lone journalist, witness to events in places throughout the world wherever action was hottest. I see this writer-hero wearing a trench coat, belted and buckled, collar turned up. Sheehan, tall, with fair Irish-American good looks; his writings, both lyrical and thoughtful, will always be, for me, the prototype of this genus.

Yet, at the conference, it was Charles Jackson who presented himself as a gift, less obviously impressive than the other two; "Chaplinesque," rather that Goethe-like or swashbuckling Romantic, he who would prove to be my close friend.

Since our relationship dated from the time following the overwhelming success of the *The Lost Weekend* and the film made from it, starring Ray Milland, I know, only by hearsay about his prior life when he was poor, writing radio soap operas and teaching, when he could find a job since he lacked the proper academic credentials. But one anecdote he used to tell about those days stays with me because it characterizes his childlike fancy, his wistfulness, his unbridled ambition and his acquisitiveness. Driving from New York City with his family to visit his wife Rhoda's parents in Vermont, they always passed, en route, three perfect eighteenth-century town houses, white shingle, with black trim and shutters, perched in a row of three on a ridge in the New Hampshire countryside.

"When papa is very rich, we will live in one of these," he promised his two small daughters and his wife.

As in the storybooks, the wish came true, for it was in Orford that I was introduced to the Jackson family. But true to its type, as the tale continued, the wish brought in its wake sorrow and frustration, for which the gracious colonial house was the setting. I remember, especially, Charlie's study, a bright, spacious room, with lavish moldings, his desk impressive enough to have been used for the signing of the Declaration of Independence, his pens, pencils, pads, typewriters, neatly ranged, were almost never touched, for in this aristocratic setting, he suffered a paralyzing writer's block. Crowded into a Greenwich Village tenement, with wife and babies, often unemployed and penniless, he had managed to compose many short stories and *The Lost Weekend* that changed his life, while in this lovely long-coveted home, he wandered idly from room to room. Was he halted by that first astonishing triumph, unable to compete with himself, or, just like the prophesy of misfortune, the *maledetto* in Verdi's opera, *Rigoletto*, did the old house harbor a curse? Charles Jackson seemed an outsider in his own home. Praising the scenic wallpaper in the dining room or the graceful arch of the stairs, he was more caretaker-guide than host. The sight of his two pretty, young daughters trudging up the hill towards home, in summer holding their prize of wild flowers, in winter, wearing ski suits—bright dots against the expanse of snow—were like illustrations from *Heidi* and *Hans Brinker and the Silver Skates*. They were possessions, also, yet Charlie, in his fashion, was a fond and sentient parent.

"I will always remember the sensation of holding in my hand that small infant's foot," he told me, with wonderment in his voice. "It was so silky and, somehow heavy, like a round stone washed smooth by waves."

Visits to Orford were often interrupted by Charlie's bouts of drinking. Sometimes, when he was locked inside his room, the life of the house would continue around him, as though nothing were happening; at other times, my husband and I would make a hurried getaway. But it was at Orford that Charlie indoctrinated me, through his record collection, into a new intimacy with music, including that quintet by Schubert, a leitmotif that has the power to this day to bring the past into the present. But reading was our chief link. We were bound together by shared admirations—fans—we retained the childlike ability to be totally absorbed, transported by a book. It was this, more than anything else, that attached me to this comic-tragic, Chaplinesque man, in a relationship, less ardent than love, more stimulating than friendship.

When he was in New York City, Charlie often stayed with us. Again these encounters were subject to uncontrolled bouts of drinking. During one visit he disappeared for several days, and his wife, over the telephone from Orford, directed me to pack his bag and to leave it in the hall next to the front door, which I did, hesitating over a full bottle of sleeping pills. But I recoiled from the role of psychiatric nurse, and I decided to include the Seconal along with his tidy shirts and argyle socks. In the afternoon the suitcase was gone and I breathed a sigh of relief. But I found the door of his room tightly shut. Although I knocked loudly and called out, there was no response. I went in. Charlie lay in bed, wearing pink pajamas, apparently asleep, but he was not to be roused. The bottle of Seconal, almost empty, was on the floor beside him; a few pills were scattered over the carpet like jewels spilled from a casket. When the ambulance arrived, they loaded Charlie onto a stretcher and I followed as they carried him out. I noted, in cold blood, that with his face partially covered by the hospital sheet, his prominent, bald forehead resembled the portraits of William Shakespeare. I was shocked by my own detachment, until it occurred to me that Charlie, had he been conscious, would have been flattered. I believe he would have chosen my notice of his likeness to the "Bard" in preference to the warmest compassion. I failed to tell him about my discovery and remembered the scene only after his death. Following a stay at Bellevue, Charlie, as usual recovered completely and returned to living with renewed zest.

Geography: the miles between Orford, New Hampshire, and New York City separated us much of the time. One summer our families vacationed together at Nantucket, but communication between Charlie and me was carried on, largely through the obsolete function of letter writing. I see the long envelopes, fat with neatly typed pages, postscripts added at the end and the margins were garlands of afterthoughts. His signature, bold, round, legible, was a trademark like his small black mustache. The letters always began: *Chère Mme. Straus*—a jest between us—that was not altogether that, but, rather a homage to our mutual idol, the author of *Remembrance of Things Past*. Charlie and I had been delighted by the coincidence with Mme. Emil Straus, friend of Marcel Proust, Parisian salon hostess, daughter of the composer, Halevy, and widow of Bizet.

In his copious letters, he waxed more brilliant than in conversation, face to face. I wonder sometimes today, when letter writing is all but extinct, if Charlie, a late practitioner, kept our relationship alive through this lost art.

One summer when I had been engrossed by Thomas Mann's *The Magic Mountain*, I received an account from Charlie of his stay in Davos, where he had been sent as a young man through the bounty of a wealthy friend. Sitting at my favorite spot for reading, in our garden, in the shade of a giant maple, Charlie's letter merged with the book. It is possible that this effect was deliberate on his part, because for Charles Jackson, literature and life were never altogether separate. Despite the heat of August in Westchester, I seemed to breathe the pure, thin air of the Swiss Alps and Hans Castorp, Mann's protagonist, became one with Charlie. Not only did they share their tuberculin bacillus, but the enfeeblement of alienation as well: Castorp symbolizing the attenuation and confusion of an era's end; Charles Jackson, the insecurity of a small-town American exposed, for the first time, to the sophistication and glitter of European society. From the remove of his invalid's balcony in the sanitarium, Charlie had observed a family of sisters and brothers, approximately his own age, tall, blond, beautiful and aristocratic. He had learned that they were white

Russians in Davos for the skiing, and that they rarely mingled with the patients from the sanitarium. Despite his timidity, Charlie determined to meet them. Like a hunting dog on the scent, he informed himself of the name of each one of the glamorous sisters and brothers, their routines and rendezvous. He trailed them to the cafés in the town and, from his balcony, he followed them, as far as possible, with his gaze, along the road to the ski lift. He admired the casual fashion with which they shouldered their skis and envied their easy comaraderie. And when they moved beyond his vision, his imagination pictured them like demi-gods from Wagner's *Ring Cycle*, poised for flight on a topmost peak. At night, when he was enjoying his final open-air repose well bundled up under a black sky, crisp with frosty stars, Charlie listened to the orchestra in the ballroom of a nearby hotel, and, in his mind's eye, he saw the mythical family as they danced tirelessly into the dawn, everyone, as unaware as the characters in *The Magic Mountain* of the upheavals that were lying in wait for them. Charlie, too, did not think beyond the next day when, perhaps, he would, at last, have the good fortune to meet the Russian family, so similar, in his fancy, to the Rostovs in Tolstoy's *War and Peace*. One morning, he managed to corner his prey along a path in the pine woods used for daily exercise by the patients in the sanitarium. He stopped Elena, the youngest and loveliest of the sisters, and overcoming his shyness, he struck up a conversation with her. Not long afterwards, he was dancing, blissfully, with the little clan to the latest jazz records he had brought with him from the United States.

Some of his letter went further back, to his growing up in Newark, New York. They told of the pettiness, meanness, the limitations of the inhabitants. But Charlie, with his writer's memory, was able to magnify into high drama the pleasures, fears, victories and hopes of a small-town boyhood.

Among the last letters I received was one that differed from the rest, and I wish I had it in my possession now. But it is with his other papers and manuscripts in the library of Dartmouth College, a stone's throw from Orford. Perhaps, the letter might prove to be disappointing if it were reread after so long.

"*Chère Madame Straus*, I am writing this very late at night or, rather, in the small hours of the morning . . ."

I pictured him at his desk in his elegant federalist study. He had recovered from his writer's block, but this later work never lived up to his expectations. As he grew older, perhaps, his vitality was, at last, drained by his excesses and the highwire act of his nature, both genteel and outrageous.

The letter began with domestic news: Sarah (his older daughter) had been home for the weekend, she would graduate in the spring; then, what? Charlie worried . . .

Sarah had her mother's personality, stable, literal-minded, but her dusky beauty derived from her father's side of the family. Although Charlie tried not to show it, Sarah was his favorite and he delighted in repeating her precise, unimaginative remarks. Kate, his younger daughter, was fair, with her mother's light blue eyes, but her father bequeathed to her his love of books and his warmth.

The letter went on to complain about his wife's stinginess. It was her Scottish blood. She refused to buy a new dress, even though he threatened to throw the old one into the garbage can. Sheila, their boxer dog, had had an unfortunate spat with a porcupine and her body had as many quills as there are feathers in an Indian chief's headdress. Suddenly, there was a change of tone. For several weeks he had been thinking about a work sparked by Pushkin's narrative poem *Eugen Onegin*.

I am going to try it out on you, he wrote.

Had he been listening to the opera on his phonograph? Or was the impulse fueled by alcohol? I visualized him on a magic carpet, floating through the dark panes of the library window, flying above the New England landscape where nothing stirred, arriving at a *dacha* outside Moscow. Tatiana sits in her garden waiting for a response from the haughty, disdainful Eugen Onegin to her love letter penned through the night before. As I read on, I saw that I had been mistaken: the scene of Charles Jackson's poem was home, Orford, New Hampshire; the heroine, his own daughter, Sarah, the object of her love, an Ivy League college man. I had been aware that, in reality, Charlie disapproved of him. He had told me, "He's all wrong for her, too rich, spoiled and sophisticated."

In her bedroom, Charlie's heroine is composing her declaration of love. In this version, the old nurse is Rhoda, who promises to mail the letter at the Orford post office on her way to the supermarket. The young man appears driving an expensive sports car wearing a blazer with a Yale insignia. His manner is cool, he considers himself superior to this inexperienced country girl. Following a trip around the world by plane (shorter than Onegin's absence abroad), he returns, in love, to claim the heroine. But it is too late; she is already married to an older man.

★ ★ ★

In his wildest moods, when Charlie was very drunk, he had the audacity to believe he was one of his favorite writers. Now in a reversal of things, the worshipper of literature, a living dybbuk, invaded the imagined person of a famous corpse. When sober, depressed, he would ask, "What if I have all the liabilities of genius, without any of its inspiration?"

As I came to the end of his pastiche, I saw that although the plot and rhyme scheme were modeled upon Pushkin's poem, this work belonged to Charlie, indigenous, the product of his own heart. Tatiana, Sarah's husband, had been altered in the transposition. In place of the valorous general, in full military regalia, his broad chest decorated with medals and ribbons, there was substituted the mere suggestion of a human being. But in this blurred presentation, I was able to discern a familiar silhouette; short, plump, bald, Chaplinesque.

> Dear *Madame Straus*, let me know by return mail, what you think of this poem.
> My love, always. Your Charlie.

When the telephone rang, I was surprised to hear the voice of Charlie's agent.

"Charlie died this morning from a combination of alcohol and sleeping pills," he said.

His health had been poor for several months and he was living at the Chelsea Hotel in New York City, with a friend. He had not been alone in the apartment at the time of his death—was it suicide or sham? More likely neither;

but rather his exhausted body could no longer tolerate the habitual doses. As I hung up, I felt more stunned and disbelieving than sorrowful. I could not give credence to the fact that Charlie was gone: This act had been played so often, and, always, my friend had been restored, rosy and energetic. I could not accept his death; later I missed him, sorely, and then the anodyne of forgetfulness set in. I do not even know where he is buried. But now, that memory has revived him once again, his remains, do not seem to be located in the dead community of a cemetery. His memorial is to be found in the papery conservation of letters, stored in a college library, a stone's throw from Orford, New Hampshire.

CODA

The *Overture* to *Swann's Way* in *A la recherche du temps perdu* by
Marcel Proust presents a scene to which I return again and
again. I identify with the daguerrotype of this nineteenth-
century French bourgeois family seated around an iron table in
front of the house in Cambray, in a garden sheltered by a big
chestnut tree. It is dinner time and the group—mother, a
tender, cultivated, wealthy Jewess, upwardly mobile father,
from peasant stock, the maternal grandmother, addicted to the
letters of Mme. de Sevigné and the Nature prescriptions of
Jean-Jacques Rousseau, the grandfather, sundry great aunts
and the narrator, Marcel, as a small boy—are awaiting a guest.
It is Swann, their neighbor, a Parisian man-about-town, who
is about to invade their hermetic nest.

> . . . we heard from the far end of the garden, not the shrill
> alarm bell, which assailed with its ferrogenous, interminable
> frozen sound any member of the household who set it off
> "without ringing," but the double tinkle, timid, oval, golden
> of the visitors bell . . .*

Remembrance of Things Past, Vol. 1, *Swann's Way*, Marcel Proust
translated by C. K. Scott Moncrieff, Chatto and Windus, London, 1992.

But it is only an instant of suspended motion. Soon the narrator animates the still figures and they will start into life. The resurrection of lost time has begun. But I have only to turn back to the indicated page to find them again, unchanged, in their places in the garden which is as much mine as the original one of my early childhood.

The memory of a first garden has a paradisical quality, like a primitive painting of Eden in which small details are presented, enlarged, without perspective. I see a tall rosy brick wall against which hollyhocks, ladies festively dressed as if for a ball, are supported and protected from inclement weather. Brick paths cut squares bordered by dark-eyed pansies, papery petunias and sweet Williams; well-tended children in their cribs, tucked inside tufted grass plots. A hummingbird and a butterfly pose coquettishly for their photographs, poised on the petals of a hydrangea bush, and the sky above is always colored blue.

A figure of a woman in white is sitting here, her features hidden by the wide brim of her hat, her head lowered over a book. She is Alma, my mother, and she waits for Alfred—Swann—to enter through an archway in the brick wall of the enclosed garden. I approach her, but as I draw near, her identity dissolves and, under the concealment of the brim, it is my own face that I discover.